Crucial Advances
for AI Driverless Cars

Practical Advances in Artificial Intelligence (AI) and Machine Learning

Dr. Lance B. Eliot, MBA, PhD

DEDICATION

To my incredible son, Michael, and my incredible daughter, Lauren.

Forest fortuna adiuvat (from the Latin; good fortune favors the brave).

CONTENTS

Lance B. Eliot

ACKNOWLEDGMENTS

I have been the beneficiary of advice and counsel by many friends, colleagues, family, investors, and many others. I want to thank everyone that has aided me throughout my career. I write from the heart and the head, having experienced first-hand what it means to have others around you that support you during the good times and the tough times.

To Warren Bennis, one of my doctoral advisors and ultimately a colleague, I offer my deepest thanks and appreciation, especially for his calm and insightful wisdom and support.

To Mark Stevens and his generous efforts toward funding and supporting the USC Stevens Center for Innovation.

To Lloyd Greif and the USC Lloyd Greif Center for Entrepreneurial Studies for their ongoing encouragement of founders and entrepreneurs.

To Peter Drucker, William Wang, Aaron Levie, Peter Kim, Jon Kraft, Cindy Crawford, Jenny Ming, Steve Milligan, Chis Underwood, Frank Gehry, Buzz Aldrin, Steve Forbes, Bill Thompson, Dave Dillon, Alan Fuerstman, Larry Ellison, Jim Sinegal, John Sperling, Mark Stevenson, Anand Nallathambi, Thomas Barrack, Jr., and many other innovators and leaders that I have met and gained mightily from doing so.

Thanks to Ed Trainor, Kevin Anderson, James Hickey, Wendell Jones, Ken Harris, DuWayne Peterson, Mike Brown, Jim Thornton, Abhi Beniwal, Al Biland, John Nomura, Eliot Weinman, John Desmond, and many others for their unwavering support during my career.

And most of all thanks as always to Lauren and Michael, for their ongoing support and for having seen me writing and heard much of this material during the many months involved in writing it. To their patience and willingness to listen.

Lance B. Eliot

INTRODUCTION

This is a book that provides the newest innovations and the latest Artificial Intelligence (AI) advances about the emerging nature of AI-based autonomous self-driving driverless cars. Via recent advances in Artificial Intelligence (AI) and Machine Learning (ML), we are nearing the day when vehicles can control themselves and will not require and nor rely upon human intervention to perform their driving tasks (or, that <u>allow</u> for human intervention, but only *require* human intervention in very limited ways).

Similar to my other related books, which I describe in a moment and list the chapters in the Appendix A of this book, I am particularly focused on those advances that pertain to self-driving cars. The phrase "autonomous vehicles" is often used to refer to any kind of vehicle, whether it is ground-based or in the air or sea, and whether it is a cargo hauling trailer truck or a conventional passenger car. Though the aspects described in this book are certainly applicable to all kinds of autonomous vehicles, I am focused more so here on cars.

Indeed, I am especially known for my role in aiding the advancement of self-driving cars, serving currently as the Executive Director of the Cybernetic Self-Driving Cars Institute.. In addition to writing software, designing and developing systems and software for self-driving cars, I also speak and write quite a bit about the topic. This book is a collection of some of my more advanced essays. For those of you that might have seen my essays posted elsewhere, I have updated them and integrated them into this book as one handy cohesive package.

You might be interested in companion books that I have written that provide additional key innovations and fundamentals about self-driving cars. Those books are entitled **"Introduction to Driverless Self-Driving Cars," "Advances in AI and Autonomous Vehicles: Cybernetic Self-Driving Cars," "Self-Driving Cars: "The Mother of All AI Projects," "Innovation and Thought Leadership on Self-Driving Driverless Cars," "New Advances in AI Autonomous Driverless Self-Driving Cars," and "Autonomous Vehicle Driverless Self-Driving Cars and**

Artificial Intelligence" and **"Transformative Artificial Intelligence Driverless Self-Driving Cars,"** and **"Disruptive Artificial Intelligence and Driverless Self-Driving Cars,** and **"State-of-the-Art AI Driverless Self-Driving Cars,"** and **"Top Trends in AI Self-Driving Cars,"** and **"AI Innovations and Self-Driving Cars"** (they are all available via Amazon). See Appendix A of this herein book to see a listing of the chapters covered in those three books.

For the introduction here to this book, I am going to borrow my introduction from those companion books, since it does a good job of laying out the landscape of self-driving cars and my overall viewpoints on the topic. The remainder of the book is all new material that does not appear in the companion books.

INTRODUCTION TO SELF-DRIVING CARS

This is a book about self-driving cars. Someday in the future, we'll all have self-driving cars and this book will perhaps seem antiquated, but right now, we are at the forefront of the self-driving car wave. Daily news bombards us with flashes of new announcements by one car maker or another and leaves the impression that within the next few weeks or maybe months that the self-driving car will be here. A casual non-technical reader would assume from these news flashes that in fact we must be on the cusp of a true self-driving car.

Here's a real news flash: We are still quite a distance from having a true self-driving car. It is years to go before we get there.

Why is that? Because a true self-driving car is akin to a moonshot. In the same manner that getting us to the moon was an incredible feat, likewise can it be said for achieving a true self-driving car. Anybody that suggests or even brashly states that the true self-driving car is nearly here should be viewed with great skepticism. Indeed, you'll see that I often tend to use the word "hogwash" or "crock" when I assess much of the decidedly *fake news* about self-driving cars. Those of us on the inside know that what is often reported to the outside is malarkey. Few of the insiders are willing to say so. I have no such hesitation.

Indeed, I've been writing a popular blog post about self-driving cars and hitting hard on those that try to wave their hands and pretend that we are on the imminent verge of true self-driving cars. For many years, I've been known as the AI Insider. Besides writing about AI, I also develop AI software. I do what I describe. It also gives me insights into what others that are doing AI are really doing versus what it is said they are doing.

Many faithful readers had asked me to pull together my insightful short essays and put them into another book, which you are now holding in your hands.

For those of you that have been reading my essays over the years, this collection not only puts them together into one handy package, I also updated the essays and added new material. For those of you that are new to the topic of self-driving cars and AI, I hope you find these essays approachable and informative. I also tend to have a writing style with a bit of a voice, and so you'll see that I am times have a wry sense of humor and also like to poke at conformity.

As a former professor and founder of an AI research lab, I for many years wrote in the formal language of academic writing. I published in referred journals and served as an editor for several AI journals. This writing here is not of the nature, and I have adopted a different and more informal style for these essays. That being said, I also do mention from time-to-time more rigorous material on AI and encourage you all to dig into those deeper and more formal materials if so interested.

I am also an AI practitioner. This means that I write AI software for a living. Currently, I head-up the Cybernetics Self-Driving Car Institute, where we are developing AI software for self-driving cars. I am excited to also report that my son, also a software engineer, heads-up our Cybernetics Self-Driving Car Lab. What I have helped to start, and for which he is an integral part, ultimately he will carry long into the future after I have retired. My daughter, a marketing whiz, also is integral to our efforts as head of our Marketing group. She too will carry forward the legacy now being formulated.

For those of you that are reading this book and have a penchant for writing code, you might consider taking a look at the open source code available for self-driving cars. This is a handy place to start learning how to develop AI for self-driving cars. There are also many new educational courses spring forth.

There is a growing body of those wanting to learn about and develop self-driving cars, and a growing body of colleges, labs, and other avenues by which you can learn about self-driving cars.

This book will provide a foundation of aspects that I think will get you ready for those kinds of more advanced training opportunities. If you've already taken those classes, you'll likely find these essays especially interesting as they offer a perspective that I am betting few other instructors or faculty offered to you. These are challenging essays that ask you to think beyond the conventional about self-driving cars.

THE MOTHER OF ALL AI PROJECTS

In June 2017, Apple CEO Tim Cook came out and finally admitted that Apple has been working on a self-driving car. As you'll see in my essays, Apple was enmeshed in secrecy about their self-driving car efforts. We have only been able to read the tea leaves and guess at what Apple has been up to. The notion of an iCar has been floating for quite a while, and self-driving engineers and researchers have been signing tight-lipped Non-Disclosure Agreements (NDA's) to work on projects at Apple that were as shrouded in mystery as any military invasion plans might be.

Tim Cook said something that many others in the Artificial Intelligence (AI) field have been saying, namely, the creation of a self-driving car has got to be the mother of all AI projects. In other words, it is in fact a tremendous moonshot for AI. If a self-driving car can be crafted and the AI works as we hope, it means that we have made incredible strides with AI and that therefore it opens many other worlds of potential breakthrough accomplishments that AI can solve.

Is this hyperbole? Am I just trying to make AI seem like a miracle worker and so provide self-aggrandizing statements for those of us writing the AI software for self-driving cars? No, it is not hyperbole. Developing a true self-driving car is really, really, really hard to do. Let me take a moment to explain why. As a side note, I realize that the Apple CEO is known for at times uttering hyperbole, and he had previously said for example that the year 2012 was "the mother of all years," and he had said that the release of iOS 10 was "the mother of all releases" – all of which does suggest he likes to use the handy "mother of" expression. But, I assure you, in terms of true self-driving cars, he has hit the nail on the head. For sure.

When you think about a moonshot and how we got to the moon, there are some identifiable characteristics and those same aspects can be applied to creating a true self-driving car. You'll notice that I keep putting the word "true" in front of the self-driving car expression. I do so because as per my essay about the various levels of self-driving cars, there are some self-driving cars that are only somewhat of a self-driving car. The somewhat versions are ones that require a human driver to be ready to intervene. In my view, that's not a true self-driving car. A true self-driving car is one that requires no human driver intervention at all. It is a car that can entirely undertake via automation the driving task without any human driver needed. This is the essence of what is known as a Level 5 self-driving car. We are currently at the Level 2 and Level 3 mark, and not yet at Level 5.

Getting to the moon involved aspects such as having big stretch goals, incremental progress, experimentation, innovation, and so on. Let's review how this applied to the moonshot of the bygone era, and how it applies to the self-driving car moonshot of today.

Big Stretch Goal

Trying to take a human and deliver the human to the moon, and bring them back, safely, was an extremely large stretch goal at the time. No one knew whether it could be done. The technology wasn't available yet. The cost was huge. The determination would need to be fierce. Etc. To reach a Level 5 self-driving car is going to be the same. It is a big stretch goal. We can readily get to the Level 3, and we are able to see the Level 4 just up ahead, but a Level 5 is still an unknown as to if it is doable. It should eventually be doable and in the same way that we thought we'd eventually get to the moon, but when it will occur is a different story.

Incremental Progress

Getting to the moon did not happen overnight in one fell swoop. It took years and years of incremental progress to get there. Likewise for self-driving cars. Google has famously been striving to get to the Level 5, and pretty much been willing to forgo dealing with the intervening levels, but most of the other self-driving car makers are doing the incremental route. Let's get a good Level 2 and a somewhat Level 3 going. Then, let's improve the Level 3 and get a somewhat Level 4 going. Then, let's improve the Level 4 and finally arrive at a Level 5. This seems to be the prevalent way that we are going to achieve the true self-driving car.

Experimentation

You likely know that there were various experiments involved in perfecting the approach and technology to get to the moon. As per making incremental progress, we first tried to see if we could get a rocket to go into space and safety return, then put a monkey in there, then with a human, then we went all the way to the moon but didn't land, and finally we arrived at the mission that actually landed on the moon. Self-driving cars are the same way. We are doing simulations of self-driving cars. We do testing of self-driving cars on private land under controlled situations. We do testing of self-driving cars on public roadways, often having to meet regulatory requirements including for example having an engineer or equivalent in the car to take over the controls if needed. And so on. Experiments big and small are needed to figure out what works and what doesn't.

Innovation

There are already some advances in AI that are allowing us to progress toward self-driving cars. We are going to need even more advances. Innovation in all aspects of technology are going to be required to achieve a true self-driving car. By no means do we already have everything in-hand that we need to get there. Expect new inventions and new approaches, new algorithms, etc.

Setbacks

Most of the pundits are avoiding talking about potential setbacks in the progress toward self-driving cars. Getting to the moon involved many setbacks, some of which you never have heard of and were buried at the time so as to not dampen enthusiasm and funding for getting to the moon. A recurring theme in many of my included essays is that there are going to be setbacks as we try to arrive at a true self-driving car. Take a deep breath and be ready. I just hope the setbacks don't completely stop progress. I am sure that it will cause progress to alter in a manner that we've not yet seen in the self-driving car field. I liken the self-driving car of today to the excitement everyone had for Uber when it first got going. Today, we have a different view of Uber and with each passing day there are more regulations to the ride sharing business and more concerns raised. The darling child only stays a darling until finally that child acts up. It will happen the same with self-driving cars.

SELF-DRIVING CARS CHALLENGES

But what exactly makes things so hard to have a true self-driving car, you might be asking. You have seen cruise control for years and years. You've lately seen cars that can do parallel parking. You've seen YouTube videos of Tesla drivers that put their hands out the window as their car zooms along the highway, and seen to therefore be in a self-driving car. Aren't we just needing to put a few more sensors onto a car and then we'll have in-hand a true self-driving car? Nope.

Consider for a moment the nature of the driving task. We don't just let anyone at any age drive a car. Worldwide, most countries won't license a driver until the age of 18, though many do allow a learner's permit at the age of 15 or 16. Some suggest that a younger age would be physically too small to reach the controls of the car. Though this might be the case, we could easily adjust the controls to allow for younger aged and thus smaller stature. It's not their physical size that matters. It's their cognitive development that matters.

To drive a car, you need to be able to reason about the car, what the car can and cannot do. You need to know how to operate the car. You need to know about how other cars on the road drive. You need to know what is allowed in driving such as speed limits and driving within marked lanes. You need to be able to react to situations and be able to avoid getting into accidents. You need to ascertain when to hit your brakes, when to steer clear of a pedestrian, and how to keep from ramming that motorcyclist that just cut you off.

Many of us had taken courses on driving. We studied about driving and took driver training. We had to take a test and pass it to be able to drive. The point being that though most adults take the driving task for granted, and we often "mindlessly" drive our cars, there is a significant amount of cognitive effort that goes into driving a car. After a while, it becomes second nature. You don't especially think about how you drive, you just do it. But, if you watch a novice driver, say a teenager learning to drive, you suddenly realize that there is a lot more complexity to it than we seem to realize.

Furthermore, driving is a very serious task. I recall when my daughter and son first learned to drive. They are both very conscientious people. They wanted to make sure that whatever they did, they did well, and that they did not harm anyone. Every day, when you get into a car, it is probably around 4,000 pounds of hefty metal and plastics (about two tons), and it is a lethal weapon. Think about it. You drive down the street in an object that weighs two tons and with the engine it can accelerate and ram into anything you want to hit. The damage a car can inflict is very scary. Both my children were surprised that they were being given the right to maneuver this monster of a beast that could cause tremendous harm entirely by merely letting go of the steering wheel for a moment or taking your eyes off the road.

In fact, in the United States alone there are about 30,000 deaths per year by auto accidents, which is around 100 per day. Given that there are about 263 million cars in the United States, I am actually more amazed that the number of fatalities is not a lot higher. During my morning commute, I look at all the thousands of cars on the freeway around me, and I think that if all of them decided to go zombie and drive in a crazy maniac way, there would be many people dead. Somehow, incredibly, each day, most people drive relatively safely. To me, that's a miracle right there. Getting millions and millions of people to be safe and sane when behind the wheel of a two ton mobile object, it's a feat that we as a society should admire with pride.

So, hopefully you are in agreement that the driving task requires a great deal of cognition. You don't' need to be especially smart to drive a car, and we've done quite a bit to make car driving viable for even the average dolt. There isn't an IQ test that you need to take to drive a car. If you can read and write, and pass a test, you pretty much can legally drive a car. There are of course some that drive a car and are not legally permitted to do so, plus there are private areas such as farms where drivers are young, but for public roadways in the United States, you can be generally of average intelligence (or less) and be able to legally drive.

This though makes it seem like the cognitive effort must not be much. If the cognitive effort was truly hard, wouldn't we only have Einstein's that could drive a car? We have made sure to keep the driving task as simple as we can, by making the controls easy and relatively standardized, and by having roads that are relatively standardized, and so on. It is as though Disneyland has put their Autopia into the real-world, by us all as a society agreeing that roads will be a certain way, and we'll all abide by the various rules of driving.

A modest cognitive task by a human is still something that stymies AI. You certainly know that AI has been able to beat chess players and be good at other kinds of games. This type of narrow cognition is not what car driving is about. Car driving is much wider. It requires knowledge about the world, which a chess playing AI system does not need to know. The cognitive aspects of driving are on the one hand seemingly simple, but at the same time require layer upon layer of knowledge about cars, people, roads, rules, and a myriad of other "common sense" aspects. We don't have any AI systems today that have that same kind of breadth and depth of awareness and knowledge.

As revealed in my essays, the self-driving car of today is using trickery to do particular tasks. It is all very narrow in operation. Plus, it currently assumes that a human driver is ready to intervene. It is like a child that we have taught to stack blocks, but we are needed to be right there in case the child stacks them too high and they begin to fall over. AI of today is brittle, it is narrow, and it does not approach the cognitive abilities of humans. This is why the true self-driving car is somewhere out in the future.

Another aspect to the driving task is that it is not solely a mind exercise. You do need to use your senses to drive. You use your eyes a vision sensors to see the road ahead. You vision capability is like a streaming video, which your brain needs to continually analyze as you drive. Where is the road? Is there a pedestrian in the way? Is there another car ahead of you? Your senses are relying a flood of info to your brain. Self-driving cars are trying to do the same, by using cameras, radar, ultrasound, and lasers. This is an attempt at mimicking how humans have senses and sensory apparatus.

Thus, the driving task is mental and physical. You use your senses, you use your arms and legs to manipulate the controls of the car, and you use your brain to assess the sensory info and direct your limbs to act upon the controls of the car. This all happens instantly. If you've ever perhaps gotten something in your eye and only had one eye available to drive with, you suddenly realize how dependent upon vision you are. If you have a broken foot with a cast, you suddenly realize how hard it is to control the brake pedal and the accelerator. If you've taken medication and your brain is maybe sluggish, you suddenly realize how much mental strain is required to drive a car.

An AI system that plays chess only needs to be focused on playing chess. The physical aspects aren't important because usually a human moves the chess pieces or the chessboard is shown on an electronic display. Using AI for a more life-and-death task such as analyzing MRI images of patients, this again does not require physical capabilities and instead is done by examining images of bits.

Driving a car is a true life-and-death task. It is a use of AI that can easily and at any moment produce death. For those colleagues of mine that are developing this AI, as am I, we need to keep in mind the somber aspects of this. We are producing software that will have in its virtual hands the lives of the occupants of the car, and the lives of those in other nearby cars, and the lives of nearby pedestrians, etc. Chess is not usually a life-or-death matter.

Driving is all around us. Cars are everywhere. Most of today's AI applications involve only a small number of people. Or, they are behind the scenes and we as humans have other recourse if the AI messes up. AI that is driving a car at 80 miles per hour on a highway had better not mess up. The consequences are grave. Multiply this by the number of cars, if we could put magically self-driving into every car in the USA, we'd have AI running in the 263 million cars. That's a lot of AI spread around. This is AI on a massive scale that we are not doing today and that offers both promise and potential peril.

There are some that want AI for self-driving cars because they envision a world without any car accidents. They envision a world in which there is no car congestion and all cars cooperate with each other. These are wonderful utopian visions.

They are also very misleading. The adoption of self-driving cars is going to be incremental and not overnight. We cannot economically just junk all existing cars. Nor are we going to be able to affordably retrofit existing cars. It is more likely that self-driving cars will be built into new cars and that over many years of gradual replacement of existing cars that we'll see the mix of self-driving cars become substantial in the real-world.

In these essays, I have tried to offer technological insights without being overly technical in my description, and also blended the business, societal, and economic aspects too. Technologists need to consider the non-technological impacts of what they do. Non-technologists should be aware of what is being developed.

We all need to work together to collectively be prepared for the enormous disruption and transformative aspects of true self-driving cars. We all need to be involved in this mother of all AI projects.

WHAT THIS BOOK PROVIDES

What does this book provide to you? It introduces many of the key elements about self-driving cars and does so with an AI based perspective. I weave together technical and non-technical aspects, readily going from being concerned about the cognitive capabilities of the driving task and how the technology is embodying this into self-driving cars, and in the next breath I discuss the societal and economic aspects.

They are all intertwined because that's the way reality is. You cannot separate out the technology per se, and instead must consider it within the milieu of what is being invented and innovated, and do so with a mindset towards the contemporary mores and culture that shape what we are doing and what we hope to do.

WHY THIS BOOK

I wrote this book to try and bring to the public view many aspects about self-driving cars that nobody seems to be discussing.

For business leaders that are either involved in making self-driving cars or that are going to leverage self-driving cars, I hope that this book will enlighten you as to the risks involved and ways in which you should be strategizing about how to deal with those risks.

For entrepreneurs, startups and other businesses that want to enter into the self-driving car market that is emerging, I hope this book sparks your interest in doing so, and provides some sense of what might be prudent to pursue.

For researchers that study self-driving cars, I hope this book spurs your interest in the risks and safety issues of self-driving cars, and also nudges you toward conducting research on those aspects.

For students in computer science or related disciplines, I hope this book will provide you with interesting and new ideas and material, for which you might conduct research or provide some career direction insights for you.

For AI companies and high-tech companies pursuing self-driving cars, this book will hopefully broaden your view beyond just the mere coding and development needed to make self-driving cars.

For all readers, I hope that you will find the material in this book to be stimulating. Some of it will be repetitive of things you already know. But I am pretty sure that you'll also find various eureka moments whereby you'll discover a new technique or approach that you had not earlier thought of. I am also betting that there will be material that forces you to rethink some of your current practices.

I am not saying you will suddenly have an epiphany and change what you are doing. I do think though that you will reconsider or perhaps revisit what you are doing.

For anyone choosing to use this book for teaching purposes, please take a look at my suggestions for doing so, as described in the Appendix. I have found the material handy in courses that I have taught, and likewise other faculty have told me that they have found the material handy, in some cases as extended readings and in other instances as a core part of their course (depending on the nature of the class).

In my writing for this book, I have tried carefully to blend both the practitioner and the academic styles of writing. It is not as dense as is typical academic journal writing, but at the same time offers depth by going into the nuances and trade-offs of various practices.

The word "deep" is in vogue today, meaning getting deeply into a subject or topic, and so is the word "unpack" which means to tease out the underlying aspects of a subject or topic. I have sought to offer material that addresses an issue or topic by going relatively deeply into it and make sure that it is well unpacked.

Finally, in any book about AI, it is difficult to use our everyday words without having some of them be misinterpreted. Specifically, it is easy to anthropomorphize AI. When I say that an AI system "knows" something, I do not want you to construe that the AI system has sentience and "knows" in the same way that humans do. They aren't that way, as yet. I have tried to use quotes around such words from time-to-time to emphasize that the words I am using should not be misinterpreted to ascribe true human intelligence to the AI systems that we know of today. If I used quotes around all such words, the book would be very difficult to read, and so I am doing so judiciously. Please keep that in mind as you read the material, thanks.

COMPANION BOOKS

If you find this material of interest, you might want to also see my other books on self-driving cars, entitled:

1. **"Introduction to Driverless Self-Driving Cars"** by Dr. Lance Eliot

2. **"Innovation and Thought Leadership on Self-Driving Driverless Cars"** by Dr. Lance Eliot

3. **"Advances in AI and Autonomous Vehicles: Cybernetic Self-Driving Cars"** by Dr. Lance Eliot

4. ***"Self-Driving Cars: The Mother of All AI Projects"*** by Dr. Lance Eliot

5. **"New Advances in AI Autonomous Driverless Self-Driving Cars"** by Dr. Lance Eliot

6. **"Autonomous Vehicle Driverless Self-Driving Cars and Artificial Intelligence"** by Dr. Lance Eliot and Michael B. Eliot

7. **"Transformative Artificial Intelligence Driverless Self-Driving Cars"** by Dr. Lance Eliot

8. **"Disruptive Artificial Intelligence and Driverless Self-Driving Cars"** by Dr. Lance Eliot

9. "State-of-the-Art AI Driverless Self-Driving Cars" by Dr. Lance Eliot

10. **"Top Trends in AI Self-Driving Cars"** by Dr. Lance Eliot

11. **"AI Innovations and Self-Driving Cars"** by Dr. Lance Eliot

12. **"Crucial Advances for AI Driverless Cars"** by Dr. Lance Eliot

All of the above books are available on Amazon and at other major global booksellers.

CHAPTER 1

ELIOT FRAMEWORK FOR AI SELF-DRIVING CARS

CHAPTER 1

ELIOT FRAMEWORK FOR AI SELF-DRIVING CARS

This chapter is a core foundational aspect for understanding AI self-driving cars and I have used this same chapter in several of my other books to introduce the reader to essential elements of this field. Once you've read this chapter, you'll be prepared to read the rest of the material since the foundational essence of the components of autonomous AI driverless self-driving cars will have been established for you.

———

When I give presentations about self-driving cars and teach classes on the topic, I have found it helpful to provide a framework around which the various key elements of self-driving cars can be understood and organized (see diagram at the end of this chapter). The framework needs to be simple enough to convey the overarching elements, but at the same time not so simple that it belies the true complexity of self-driving cars. As such, I am going to describe the framework here and try to offer in a thousand words (or more!) what the framework diagram itself intends to portray.

The core elements on the diagram are numbered for ease of reference. The numbering does not suggest any kind of prioritization of the elements. Each element is crucial. Each element has a purpose, and otherwise would not be included in the framework. For some self-driving cars, a particular element might be more important or somehow distinguished in comparison to other self-driving cars.

You could even use the framework to rate a particular self-driving car, doing so by gauging how well it performs in each of the elements of the framework. I will describe each of the elements, one at a time. After doing so, I'll discuss aspects that illustrate how the elements interact and perform during the overall effort of a self-driving car.

At the Cybernetic Self-Driving Car Institute, we use the framework to keep track of what we are working on, and how we are developing software that fills in what is needed to achieve Level 5 self-driving cars.

D-01: Sensor Capture

Let's start with the one element that often gets the most attention in the press about self-driving cars, namely, the sensory devices for a self-driving car.

On the framework, the box labeled as D-01 indicates "Sensor Capture" and refers to the processes of the self-driving car that involve collecting data from the myriad of sensors that are used for a self-driving car. The types of devices typically involved are listed, such as the use of mono cameras, stereo cameras, LIDAR devices, radar systems, ultrasonic devices, GPS, IMU, and so on.

These devices are tasked with obtaining data about the status of the self-driving car and the world around it. Some of the devices are continually providing updates, while others of the devices await an indication by the self-driving car that the device is supposed to collect data. The data might be first transformed in some fashion by the device itself, or it might instead be fed directly into the sensor capture as raw data. At that point, it might be up to the sensor capture processes to do transformations on the data. This all varies depending upon the nature of the devices being used and how the devices were designed and developed.

D-02: Sensor Fusion

Imagine that your eyeballs receive visual images, your nose receives odors, your ears receive sounds, and in essence each of your distinct sensory devices is getting some form of input. The input befits the nature of the device. Likewise, for a self-driving car, the cameras provide visual images, the radar returns radar reflections, and so on.

Each device provides the data as befits what the device does.

At some point, using the analogy to humans, you need to merge together what your eyes see, what your nose smells, what your ears hear, and piece it all together into a larger sense of what the world is all about and what is happening around you. Sensor fusion is the action of taking the singular aspects from each of the devices and putting them together into a larger puzzle.

Sensor fusion is a tough task. There are some devices that might not be working at the time of the sensor capture. Or, there might some devices that are unable to report well what they have detected. Again, using a human analogy, suppose you are in a dark room and so your eyes cannot see much. At that point, you might need to rely more so on your ears and what you hear. The same is true for a self-driving car. If the cameras are obscured due to snow and sleet, it might be that the radar can provide a greater indication of what the external conditions consist of.

In the case of a self-driving car, there can be a plethora of such sensory devices. Each is reporting what it can. Each might have its difficulties. Each might have its limitations, such as how far ahead it can detect an object. All of these limitations need to be considered during the sensor fusion task.

D-03: Virtual World Model

For humans, we presumably keep in our minds a model of the world around us when we are driving a car. In your mind, you know that the car is going at say 60 miles per hour and that you are on a freeway. You have a model in your mind that your car is surrounded by other cars, and that there are lanes to the freeway. Your model is not only based on what you can see, hear, etc., but also what you know about the nature of the world. You know that at any moment that car ahead of you can smash on its brakes, or the car behind you can ram into your car, or that the truck in the next lane might swerve into your lane.

The AI of the self-driving car needs to have a virtual world model, which it then keeps updated with whatever it is receiving from the sensor fusion, which received its input from the sensor capture and the sensory devices.

D-04: System Action Plan

By having a virtual world model, the AI of the self-driving car is able to keep track of where the car is and what is happening around the car. In addition, the AI needs to determine what to do next. Should the self-driving car hit its brakes? Should the self-driving car stay in its lane or swerve into the lane to the left? Should the self-driving car accelerate or slow down?

A system action plan needs to be prepared by the AI of the self-driving car. The action plan specifies what actions should be taken. The actions need to pertain to the status of the virtual world model. Plus, the actions need to be realizable.

This realizability means that the AI cannot just assert that the self-driving car should suddenly sprout wings and fly. Instead, the AI must be bound by whatever the self-driving car can actually do, such as coming to a halt in a distance of X feet at a speed of Y miles per hour, rather than perhaps asserting that the self-driving car come to a halt in 0 feet as though it could instantaneously come to a stop while it is in motion.

D-05: Controls Activation

The system action plan is implemented by activating the controls of the car to act according to what the plan stipulates. This might mean that the accelerator control is commanded to increase the speed of the car. Or, the steering control is commanded to turn the steering wheel 30 degrees to the left or right.

One question arises as to whether or not the controls respond as they are commanded to do. In other words, suppose the AI has commanded the accelerator to increase, but for some reason it does not do so. Or, maybe it tries to do so, but the speed of the car does not increase. The controls activation feeds back into the virtual world model, and simultaneously the virtual world model is getting updated from the sensors, the sensor capture, and the sensor fusion. This allows the AI to ascertain what has taken place as a result of the controls being commanded to take some kind of action.

By the way, please keep in mind that though the diagram seems to have a linear progression to it, the reality is that these are all aspects of the self-driving car that are happening in parallel and simultaneously. The sensors are capturing data, meanwhile the sensor fusion is taking place, meanwhile the virtual model is being updated, meanwhile the system action plan is being formulated and reformulated, meanwhile the controls are being activated.

This is the same as a human being that is driving a car. They are eyeballing the road, meanwhile they are fusing in their mind the sights, sounds, etc., meanwhile their mind is updating their model of the world around them, meanwhile they are formulating an action plan of what to do, and meanwhile they are pushing their foot onto the pedals and steering the car. In the normal course of driving a car, you are doing all of these at once. I mention this so that when you look at the diagram, you will think of the boxes as processes that are all happening at the same time, and not as though only one happens and then the next.

They are shown diagrammatically in a simplistic manner to help comprehend what is taking place. You though should also realize that they are working in parallel and simultaneous with each other. This is a tough aspect in that the inter-element communications involve latency and other aspects that must be taken into account. There can be delays in one element updating and then sharing its latest status with other elements.

D-06: Automobile & CAN

Contemporary cars use various automotive electronics and a Controller Area Network (CAN) to serve as the components that underlie the driving aspects of a car. There are Electronic Control Units (ECU's) which control subsystems of the car, such as the engine, the brakes, the doors, the windows, and so on.

The elements D-01, D-02, D-03, D-04, D-05 are layered on top of the D-06, and must be aware of the nature of what the D-06 is able to do and not do.

D-07: In-Car Commands

Humans are going to be occupants in self-driving cars. In a Level 5 self-driving car, there must be some form of communication that takes place between the humans and the self-driving car. For example, I go into a self-driving car and tell it that I want to be driven over to Disneyland, and along the way I want to stop at In-and-Out Burger. The self-driving car now parses what I've said and tries to then establish a means to carry out my wishes.

In-car commands can happen at any time during a driving journey. Though my example was about an in-car command when I first got into my self-driving car, it could be that while the self-driving car is carrying out the journey that I change my mind. Perhaps after getting stuck in traffic, I tell the self-driving car to forget about getting the burgers and just head straight over to the theme park. The self-driving car needs to be alert to in-car commands throughout the journey.

D-08: VX2 Communications

We will ultimately have self-driving cars communicating with each other, doing so via V2V (Vehicle-to-Vehicle) communications. We will also have self-driving cars that communicate with the roadways and other aspects of the transportation infrastructure, doing so via V2I (Vehicle-to-Infrastructure).

The variety of ways in which a self-driving car will be communicating with other cars and infrastructure is being called V2X, whereby the letter X means whatever else we identify as something that a car should or would want to communicate with. The V2X communications will be taking place simultaneous with everything else on the diagram, and those other elements will need to incorporate whatever it gleans from those V2X communications.

D-09: Deep Learning

The use of Deep Learning permeates all other aspects of the self-driving car. The AI of the self-driving car will be using deep learning to do a better job at the systems action plan, and at the controls activation, and at the sensor fusion, and so on.

Currently, the use of artificial neural networks is the most prevalent form of deep learning. Based on large swaths of data, the neural networks attempt to "learn" from the data and therefore direct the efforts of the self-driving car accordingly.

D-10: Tactical AI

Tactical AI is the element of dealing with the moment-to-moment driving of the self-driving car. Is the self-driving car staying in its lane of the freeway? Is the car responding appropriately to the controls commands? Are the sensory devices working?

For human drivers, the tactical equivalent can be seen when you watch a novice driver such as a teenager that is first driving. They are focused on the mechanics of the driving task, keeping their eye on the road while also trying to properly control the car.

D-11: Strategic AI

The Strategic AI aspects of a self-driving car are dealing with the larger picture of what the self-driving car is trying to do. If I had asked that the self-driving car take me to Disneyland, there is an overall journey map that needs to be kept and maintained.

There is an interaction between the Strategic AI and the Tactical AI. The Strategic AI is wanting to keep on the mission of the driving, while the Tactical AI is focused on the particulars underway in the driving effort. If the Tactical AI seems to wander away from the overarching mission, the Strategic AI wants to see why and get things back on track. If the Tactical AI realizes that there is something amiss on the self-driving car, it needs to alert the Strategic AI accordingly and have an adjustment to the overarching mission that is underway.

D-12: Self-Aware AI

Very few of the self-driving cars being developed are including a Self-Aware AI element, which we at the Cybernetic Self-Driving Car Institute believe is crucial to Level 5 self-driving cars.

The Self-Aware AI element is intended to watch over itself, in the sense that the AI is making sure that the AI is working as intended. Suppose you had a human driving a car, and they were starting to drive erratically. Hopefully, their own self-awareness would make them realize they themselves are driving poorly, such as perhaps starting to fall asleep after having been driving for hours on end. If you had a passenger in the car, they might be able to alert the driver if the driver is starting to do something amiss. This is exactly what the Self-Aware

AI element tries to do, it becomes the overseer of the AI, and tries to detect when the AI has become faulty or confused, and then find ways to overcome the issue.

D-13: Economic

The economic aspects of a self-driving car are not per se a technology aspect of a self-driving car, but the economics do indeed impact the nature of a self-driving car. For example, the cost of outfitting a self-driving car with every kind of possible sensory device is prohibitive, and so choices need to be made about which devices are used. And, for those sensory devices chosen, whether they would have a full set of features or a more limited set of features.

We are going to have self-driving cars that are at the low-end of a consumer cost point, and others at the high-end of a consumer cost point. You cannot expect that the self-driving car at the low-end is going to be as robust as the one at the high-end. I realize that many of the self-driving car pundits are acting as though all self-driving cars will be the same, but they won't be. Just like anything else, we are going to have self-driving cars that have a range of capabilities. Some will be better than others. Some will be safer than others. This is the way of the real-world, and so we need to be thinking about the economics aspects when considering the nature of self-driving cars.

D-14: Societal

This component encompasses the societal aspects of AI which also impacts the technology of self-driving cars. For example, the famous Trolley Problem involves what choices should a self-driving car make when faced with life-and-death matters. If the self-driving car is about to either hit a child standing in the roadway, or instead ram into a tree at the side of the road and possibly kill the humans in the self-driving car, which choice should be made?

We need to keep in mind the societal aspects will underlie the AI of the self-driving car. Whether we are aware of it explicitly or not, the AI will have embedded into it various societal assumptions.

D-15: Innovation

I included the notion of innovation into the framework because we can anticipate that whatever a self-driving car consists of, it will continue to be innovated over time. The self-driving cars coming out in the next several years will undoubtedly be different and less innovative than the versions that come out in ten years hence, and so on.

Framework Overall

For those of you that want to learn about self-driving cars, you can potentially pick a particular element and become specialized in that aspect. Some engineers are focusing on the sensory devices. Some engineers focus on the controls activation. And so on. There are specialties in each of the elements.

Researchers are likewise specializing in various aspects. For example, there are researchers that are using Deep Learning to see how best it can be used for sensor fusion. There are other researchers that are using Deep Learning to derive good System Action Plans. Some are studying how to develop AI for the Strategic aspects of the driving task, while others are focused on the Tactical aspects.

A well-prepared all-around software developer that is involved in self-driving cars should be familiar with all of the elements, at least to the degree that they know what each element does. This is important since whatever piece of the pie that the software developer works on, they need to be knowledgeable about what the other elements are doing.

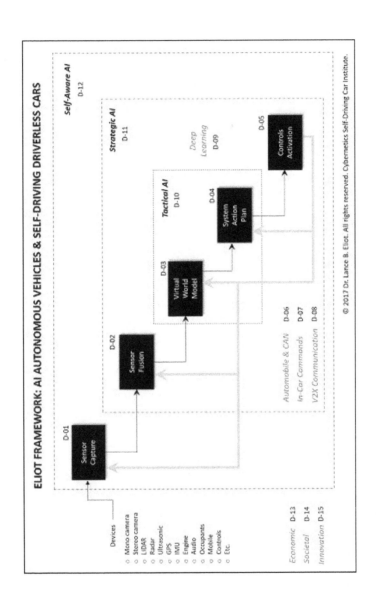

ELIOT FRAMEWORK: AI AUTONOMOUS VEHICLES & SELF-DRIVING DRIVERLESS CARS

CHAPTER 2

ENSEMBLE LEARNING AND AI SELF-DRIVING CARS

CHAPTER 2

ENSEMBLE LEARNING AND AI SELF-DRIVING CARS

How do you learn something?

That's the same question that we need to ask when trying to achieve Machine Learning (ML). In what way can we undertake "learning" for a computer and seek to "teach" the system to do things of an intelligent nature. That's a holy grail for those in AI that are aiming to avoid having to program their way into intelligent behavior. Instead, the notion is to be able to somehow get a computer to learn what to do and not need to explicitly write out every step or knowledge aspect required.

Allow me a moment to share with you a story about the nature of learning.

Earlier in my career, I started out as a professor and was excited to teach classes for both undergraduate students and graduate level students. Those first few lectures were my chance to aid those students in learning about computer science and AI. Before each lecture I spent a lot of time to prepare my lecture notes and was ready to fill the classroom whiteboard with all the key principles they'd need to know. Sure enough, I'd stride into the classroom and start writing on the board and kept doing so until the bell went off that the class session was finished.

After doing this for about a week or two, a student came to my office hours and asked if there was a textbook they could use to study from. I was taken aback since I had purposely not chosen a textbook in order to save the students money. I figured that my copious notes on the board would be better than some stodgy textbook and averted them from having to spend a fortune on costly books. The student explained that though they welcomed my approach, they were the type of person that found it easier to learn by reading a book. Trying not to offend me, the student gingerly inquired as to whether my lecture notes could be augmented by a textbook.

I considered this suggestion and sure enough found a textbook that I thought would be pretty good to recommend, and at the next session of the class mentioned it to the students, indicating that it was optional and not mandatory for the class.

While walking across the campus after a class session, another student came up to me and asked if there were any videos of my lectures. I was suspicious that the student wanted to skip coming to lecture and figured they could just watch a video instead, but this student sincerely convinced me that she found that watching a video allowed her to start and stop the lecture while trying to study the material after class sessions. She said that my fast pace during class didn't allow time for her to really soak in the points and that by having a video she would be able to do so at a measured pace on her own time.

I considered this suggestion and provided to the class links to some videos that were pertinent to the lectures that I was giving.

Yet another student came to see me about another facet of my classes. For the undergrad lectures, I spoke the entire time and didn't allow for any classroom discussion or interaction. This seemed sensible because the classes were large lecture halls that had hundreds of students attending. I figured it would not be feasible to carry on a Socratic dialogue similar to what I was doing in the graduate level courses where I had many 15-20 students per class. I had even been told by some of the senior faculty that trying to engage undergrads in discussion was a waste of time anyway since those newbie students were neophytes and it would be ineffective to allow any kind of Q&A with them.

Well, an undergrad student came to see me and asked if I was ever going to allow Q&A during my lectures. When I started to discuss this with the student, I inquired as to what kinds of questions was he thinking of asking. Turns out that we had a very vigorous back-and-forth on some meaty aspects of AI and it made me realize that there were perhaps students in the lecture hall that could indeed engage in a hearty dialogue during class. At my next lecture, I opted to stop every twenty minutes and gauge the reaction from the students and see if I could get a brief and useful interaction going with them. It worked, and I noticed that many of the students became much more interested in the lectures by this added feature of allowing for Q&A (even for so-called "lowly" undergraduate students, which was how my fellow faculty seemed to think of them).

Why do I tell you this story about my initial days of being a professor?

I found out pretty quickly that using only one method or approach to learning is not necessarily very wise. My initial impetus to do fast paced all-spoken lectures was perhaps sufficient for some students, but not for all. Furthermore, even the students that were OK with that narrow singular approach were likely to tap into other means of learning if I was able to provide it. By augmenting my lectures with videos, with textbooks, and by allowing for in-classroom discussion, I was providing a multitude of means to learn.

You'll be happy to know that I learned that learning is best done via offering multiple ways to learn. Allow the learner to select which approach best fits to them. When I say this, also keep in mind that the situation might determine which mode is best at that time. In other words, don't assume that someone that prefers learning via in-person lecture is always going to find that to be the best learning method for them. They might switch to a preference for say video or textbook, depending upon the circumstance.

And, don't assume that each learner will learn via only one method.

Student A might find that using lectures and the textbook is their best fit. Student B might find lectures to be unsuitable for learning and prefer dialogue and videos. Each learner will have their own one-or-more learning approaches that work best for them, and this varies by the nature of the topic being learned.

I kept all of this in mind for the rest of my professorial days and always tried to provide multiple learning methods to the students, so they could choose the best fit for them.

A phrase sometimes used to refer to this notion of multiple learning methods is known as ensemble learning. When you consider the word "ensemble" you tend to think of multiples of something, such as multiple musicians in an orchestra or multiple actors in a play. They each have their own role, and yet they also combine together to create a whole.

Ensemble machine learning is the same kind of concept. Rather than using only one method or approach to "teach" a computer to do something, we might use multiple methods or approaches. These multiple methods or approaches are intended to somehow ultimately work together so as to form a group. In other words, we don't want the learning methods to be so disparate that they don't end-up working together. It's like musicians that are supposed to play the same song together. The hope is that the multiple learning methods are going to lead to a greater chance at having the learner learn, which in this case is the computer system as the learner.

At the Cybernetic AI Self-Driving Car Institute, we are using ensemble machine learning as part of our approach to developing AI for self-driving cars.

Allow me to further elaborate.

Suppose I was trying to get a computer system to learn some aspect of how to drive a car. One approach might be to use artificial neural networks (ANN). This is very popular and a relatively standardized way to "teach" the computer about certain driving task aspects. That's just one approach though. I might also try to use genetic algorithms

(GA). I might also use support vector machines (SVM). And so on. These could be done in an ensemble manner, meaning that I'm trying to "teach" the same thing but using multiple learning techniques to do so.

Now you don't normally just toss together an ensemble. When you put together a musical band, you probably would be astute to pick musicians that have particular musical skills and play particular musical instruments. You'd want them to end-up being complimentary with each other. Sure, some might be duplicative, such as you might have more than one guitar player, but that could be because one guitarist will be the lead guitar and the other perhaps the bass guitar player.

The same is said for doing ensemble machine learning. You'll want to select machine learning approaches or methods that seem to make sense when considered in the totality as a group of such machine learning approaches. What is the strength of each ML chosen for the ensemble? What is the weakness of the ML chosen? By having multiple learning methods, hopefully you'll be able to either find the "best" one for the given learning circumstance at hand, or you might be able to combine them together in a manner that offers a synergistic outcome beyond each of them performing individually.

So, you could select some N number of machine learning approaches, train them on some data, and then see which of them learned the best, as based on some kind of metrics. You might after training feed the MLs with new data and see which does the best job. For example, suppose I'm trying to train toward being able to discern street signs. So, I feed a bunch of pictures of street signs into these each ML's of my ensemble. After they've each used their own respective learning approach, I then test them. I do so by feeding new pictures of street signs and see which of them most consistently can identify a stop sign versus a speed limit sign.

Out of my N number of machine learning approaches that I selected for this street sign learning task, suppose that the SVM turns out to be the "best" as based on my testing after the learning has occurred. I might then decide that for the street sign interpretation I'm going to exclusively use SVM for my AI self-driving car system. This aspect of selecting a particular model out of a set of models is sometimes referred to as the "bucket of models" approach, wherein you have a bucket of models in the ensemble and you choose one out of them. Your selection is based on a kind of "bake-off" as to which is the better choice.

But, suppose that I discover that of the N machine learning approaches, sometimes the SVM is the "best" and meanwhile there are other times that the GA is better. I don't necessarily need to confine myself to choosing only one of the learning methods for the system. What I might do is opt to use both SVM and GA, and be aware beforehand of when each is preferred to come to play. This is akin to having the two guitarists in my musical band, and each has their own strengths and weaknesses, so if I'm thoughtful about how to arrange my band when they play a concert I'll put them each into a part of the music playing that seems best for their capabilities. Maybe one of them starts the song, and the other ends the song. Or however arranging them seems most suitable to their capabilities.

Thus, we might choose N number of machine learning approaches for our ensemble, train them, and then decide that some subset Q are chosen to become part of the actual system we are putting together. Q might be 1, in that maybe there's only one of the machine learning approaches that seemed appropriate to move forward with, or Q might be 2, or 3, and so on up to the number N. If we do select more than just one, the question then arises as to when and how to use the Q number of chosen machine learning approaches.

In some cases, you might use each separately, such as maybe machine learning approach Q1 is good at detecting stop signs, while Q2 is good at detecting speed limit signs. Therefore, you put Q1 and Q2 into the real system and when it is working you are going to rely upon Q1 for stop sign detection and Q2 for speed limit sign detection.

In other cases, you might decide to combine together the machine learning approaches that have been successful to get into the set Q. I might decide that whenever a street sign is being analyzed, I'll see what Q1 has to indicate about it, and what Q2 has to indicate about it. If they both agree that it is a stop sign, I'll be satisfied that it's likely a stop sign, and especially if Q1 is very sure of it. If they both agree that it is speed limit sign, and especially if Q2 is very sure of it, I'll then be comfortable assuming that it is a speed limit sign.

There are various ways you might combine together the Q's. You could simply consider them all equal in terms of their voting power, which is generally called "bagging" or bootstrap aggregation. Or, you could consider them to be unequal in their voting power. In this case, we're going with the idea that Q1 is better at stop sign detection, so I'll add a weighting to its results that if it's interpretation is a stop sign then I'll give it a lot of weight, while if Q2 detects a stop sign I'll give it a lower weighting because I already know beforehand it's not so good at stop sign detection.

These machine learning approaches that are chosen for the ensemble are often referred to as individual learners. You can have any N number of these individual learners and it all depends on what you are trying to achieve and how many machine learning approaches you want to consider for the matter at-hand. Some also refer to these individual learners as base learners. A base or individual learner can be whatever machine learning approach you know and are comfortable with, and that matches to the learning task at hand, and as mentioned earlier can be ANN, SVM, GA, decision trees, etc.

Some believe that to make the learning task fair, you should provide essentially the same training data to the machine learning approaches that you've chosen for the matter at-hand. Thus, I might select one sample of training data that I feed into each of the N machine learning approaches. I then see how each of those machine learning approaches did based on the sample data. For example, I select a thousand street sign images and feed them into my N machine learning approaches which in this case I've chosen say three, ANN, SVM, GA.

Or, instead, I might take a series of samples of the training data. Let's refer to one such sample as S1, consisting of a thousand images randomly chosen from a population of 50,000 images, and feed the sample S1 into machine learning approach Q1. I might then select another sample of training data, let's call it S2, consisting of another randomly selected set of a thousand images, and feed it into machine learning approach Q2. And so on for each of the N machine learning approaches that I've selected.

I could then see how each of the machine learning approaches did on their respective sample data. I might then opt to keep all of the machine learning approaches for my actual system, or I might selectively choose which ones will go into my actual system. And, as mentioned earlier, if I have selected multiple machine learning approaches for the actual system then I'll want to figure out how to possibly combine together their results.

You can further advance the ensemble learning technique by adding learning upon learning. Suppose I have a base set of individual learners. I might feed their results into a second-level of machine learning approaches that act as meta-learners. In a sense, you can use the first-level to do some initial screening and scanning, and then potentially have a second-level that then aims at getting into further refinement of what the first-level found. For example, suppose my first-level identified that a street sign is a speed limit sign, but the first-level isn't capable to then determine what the speed limit numbers are. I might feed the results into a second-level that is adept at ascertaining the numbers on the speed limit sign and be able to detect what the actual speed limit is as posted on the sign.

The ensemble approach to machine learning allows for a lot of flexibility in how you undertake it. There's no particular standardized way in which you are supposed to do ensemble machine learning. It's an area still evolving as to what works best and how to most effectively and efficiently use it.

Some might be tempted to throw every machine learning approach into an ensemble under the blind hope that it will then showcase which is the best for your matter at-hand. This is not as easy as it seems. You need to know what the machine learning approach does and there's an effort involved in setting it up and giving it a fair chance. In essence, there are costs to undertaking this and you shouldn't be using a scattergun style way of doing so.

For any particular matter, there are going to be so-called weak learners and strong learners. Some of the machine learning approaches are very good in some situations and quite poor in others. You also need to be thinking about the generalizability of the machine learning approaches. You could be fooled when feeding sample data into the machine learning approaches that say one of them looks really good, but it turns out maybe it has overfitted to the sample data. This might not then do you much good once you start feeding new data into the mix.

Another aspect is the value of diversity. If you have no-diversity, such as only one machine learning approach that you are using, there are likely to be situations wherein it isn't as good as some other machine learning approach, and you should consider having diversity. Therefore, by having more than one machine learning approach in your mix, you are gaining diversity which will hopefully pay-off for varying circumstances. As with anything else, if you have too many though of the machine learning approaches it can lead to muddled results and you might not be able to know which one to believe for a given result provided.

Keep in mind that any ensemble that you put together will require computational effort, in essence computing power, in order to not only do the training but more importantly when involved in receiving new data and responding accordingly. Thus, if you opt to have a slew of machine learning approaches that are going to become part of your Q final set, and if you are expecting them to run in real-time on-board an AI self-driving car, this is going to be something you need to carefully assess. The amount of memory consumed and the processing power consumed might be prohibitive. There's a big difference between using an ensemble for a research-oriented task, wherein you might not have any particular time constraints, and versus when using in an AI self-driving car that has severe time constraints and also limits on computational processing available.

For those of you familiar with Python, you might consider trying using the Python-oriented scikit-learn machine learning library and try out various ensemble machine learning aspects to get an understanding of how to use an ensemble learning approach.

If we're going to have true AI systems, and especially AI self-driving cars, the odds are that we'll need to deploy multiple machine learning models. Trying to only program directly our way to full AI is unlikely to be feasible. As Benjamin Franklin is famous for saying: "Tell me and I forget. Teach me and I remember. Involve me and I learn." Using an ensemble learning approach is to-date a vital technique to get us toward that involve me and learn goal. We might still need even better machine learning models, but the chances are that no matter what we discover for better ML's, we'll end-up needing to combine them into an ensemble. That's how the music will come out sounding robust and fulfilling for achieving ultimate AI.

CHAPTER 3

GHOSTS IN
AI SELF-DRIVING CARS

CHAPTER 3

GHOSTS IN
AI SELF-DRIVING CARS

Ghosts. Real or not?

There's a hotel in San Diego, California that supposedly has a ghost that appears from time-to-time and has reportedly been seen by guests as it floats throughout the halls of the hotel. I went there for a computer industry conference and, due to my serving on the organizing board for the event, I got to know the hotel staff. When I asked about the alleged ghost, they were at first reluctant to talk about it. Turns out that it wasn't something that the hotel management wanted to necessarily promote and it was hoped that public would just stop asking about the ghost.

I eventually found out that the story about the ghost was based on the early history of the hotel. Supposedly, when the hotel was first being built, there was a dispute between two male construction workers about a woman they were both seeing. The story is that one of those construction workers killed the other, doing so inside the hotel prior to its completion, and snuck the body into a dirt hole that had been made for a new swimming pool. The swimming pool was ultimately finished up and the body was now hidden from view.

Years later, the swimming pool began to show some cracks and it was dug up to be resurfaced. Guess what, the remains of a dead body were found! Meanwhile, guests of the hotel had been reporting for

43

years that they would sometimes see an apparition of a male floating throughout the hotel. Wow, ghost sightings, coupled with a story that could explain the basis for the ghost. Perfect. The hotel staff then explained that the construction worker was killed in a specific room of the hotel and that it was reported that guests would sometimes hear eerie sounds in that particular room, plus, that the image of the ghost would often appear there first whenever a sighting happened and then would float throughout the rest of hotel.

One way or another, I had to stay in that room. I asked the hotel staff if I could book my room for the computer industry event to be that ghostly haunted room. They said yes. I told friends and colleagues about it. Some wondered if I would be frightened by the appearance of the ghost, if it so appeared. I told them I would be ecstatic to actually see a ghost. I began to wonder though if my friends and colleagues might try to trick me by purposely arranging for some kind of creepy sounds or lighting to fool me into believing a ghost was there. Anyway, after getting all excited about the prospects of seeing a ghost, I must report to you that with regrettable sadness and disappointment, and after having been in the room for the entire week of the conference, I did not see the ghost. Not even once. Darn!

Does the fact that I did not see the ghost therefore prove that the ghost does not exist? No, of course not. The lack of seeing the ghost doesn't proof much of anything. For those that insist ghosts exist, presumably they need to showcase that there is a ghost. But, it doesn't mean that they have to make it appear on demand. For those that insist ghosts don't exist, the mere absence of a ghost cannot prove that it cannot exist, and only suggests that at that time and place there wasn't apparently a ghost (assuming even that the ghost would be seen by our normal senses of sight, etc.).

Now, don't get me wrong and think that I'm agreeing that ghosts do exist. All I can say is that I've not yet personally experienced a ghost. Furthermore, other people that claim they've seen a ghost, well, it just seems questionable, but anyway, I'm keeping my mind open that maybe there are ghosts, and at the same time maybe there are not ghosts.

Speaking of ghosts, have you ever been using your laptop or desktop computer and it suddenly did something untoward or oddball-like that led you to exclaim that maybe a ghost was in it (or, perhaps similar evil spirits)?

In such a case, I think we might all agree that the word "ghost" is being used in a more real-world way. It's unlikely that you believe that an actual apparition of a ghostly figure opted to invade your computer and mess with it. Instead, you are suggesting that something mysterious occurred and that it happened without any apparent rhyme or reason. And, lacking a rational explanation for it, you ascribe that it was caused by some inexplicable reason.

Thus, you use the word "ghost" as a convenient placeholder. It succinctly conveys that you don't know what caused the problem and furthermore usually means that it happens intermittently. If something was happening with apparent and predictable regularity, you'd probably believe there was some systemic reason for it. By the matter happening intermittently, seemingly randomly, it gets tossed into the ghost category.

I've managed numerous help desk crews during my former years as a computer team manager and many of the help desk specialists see themselves as ghostbusters. End-users will often report that some ghost-like issue has occurred in their computer and want the help desk staff to find the ghost and get rid of it. This is more so reported by end-users that often don't know much about computers. They lack the vocabulary and technical wherewithal to otherwise ferret out the problem, and so it is easy to just say that a ghost has appeared. Some help desk staff even wear ghostbuster shirts or buttons, jokingly taking on the role of ghost finder, ghost remover, and ghost aftermath fixer of technology.

Perhaps you've experienced a ghost in your car. Ever had your car suddenly hiccup while the engine is idling at a red light? I'm guessing you've had this happen. Eerily, it happens just once, and doesn't repeat. What happened, you might ponder? What suddenly caused it? There didn't seem to be any apparent reason for it to occur. And, whatever it is, it only appeared once. Bizarre. That's likely what goes through your mind. You then also start to worry that suppose it's something serious. Maybe this is just the first indicator. Suppose it happens again and in a situation that might be direr. Or, should you just shrug it off as a fluke. Maybe it's not worth worrying about.

Those pesky ghosts!

What does this have to do with AI self-driving cars?

At the Cybernetic AI Self-Driving Car Institute, we are developing AI software for self-driving cars, and along the way we've been coming up with ways to deal with ghosts.

Yikes, ghosts in AI self-driving cars? This might seem like a scary possibility. There are some AI self-driving car pundits that keep portraying AI self-driving cars as though they are perfect and will never have any problems. It's kind of wild that anyone would think this. A self-driving car is still a car. We all know that cars have problems. Parts wear out and things break. We also all know that sometimes a car design or the parts chosen for the car can have flaws, and there are often vehicle recalls related to design elements or parts of the car. Let's all be realistic and realize that AI self-driving cars are going to have problems.

Not only will the self-driving car experience physical problems that are manifested by parts wearing out or breaking, but there's also the software that's involved in a self-driving car that will have issues too. The AI system is a complex and convoluted set of software components. Invariably, there are going to be bugs in the AI system. We already know that bugs and other software maladies have occurred in a wide range of complex systems such as those designed and developed for spacecraft, for airplanes, and a slew of similar kinds of real-time based systems. There's no special reason that an AI self-driving car will be an exception and somehow never experience a bug.

I know that some AI self-driving car pundits shake-off the potential of bugs by saying that the use of OTA will deal with it. OTA or Over The Air refers to the self-driving car having an electronic communications capability to connect typically with a cloud based system that provides updates to the self-driving car. Thus, in theory, if a bug is found in the on-board systems of the self-driving car, the auto maker or tech firm can prepare a software fix and push the fix down into the self-driving car's AI system. This is certainly logical and feasible, but it also falsely suggests that bugs aren't going to occur (they will), and the OTA is really more about being able to (hopefully) quickly ensure that a fix is put in place and has little to do with eliminating bugs.

When I refer to bugs, let's switch the terminology and refer to these anomalies as ghosts.

I'm guessing that we'll likely have self-driving car owners and occupants that are going to be reporting that there are ghosts in their AI self-driving cars. This is akin to reporting that a ghost is in your laptop or desktop computer. It's akin to when your conventional car hiccups at the red light and you blame it on a ghost.

You'll be in an AI self-driving car and something will happen that seems unexpected and mysterious, for which the easiest way to describe it is by saying that it had a ghost. Again, it's unlikely many people will genuinely believe that an evil spirit was in the AI self-driving car and they are just using the convenience of saying it was a ghost to depict that it happened out-of-the-blue. Ghosts are going to be reportedly detected in AI self-driving cars, I can guarantee it.

Who will be the AI self-driving car ghostbusters?

Presumably, the auto maker or tech firm will have ghostbusters. In addition, the companies that do maintenance and support for AI self-driving cars will likely need ghostbusters. The ghostbusters in the field will at times not necessarily be able to figure out what the ghost is. They will possibly need to confer with the auto maker or tech firm. Likewise, the auto maker or tech firm might not be able to readily figure out the ghost and will rely upon or need to have some ghostbusters in the field to assist.

You might be aware that ghosts have already been encountered in cars that are somewhat like self-driving cars. First, be aware that self-driving cars are categorized by levels of capabilities. The topmost self-driving car is a Level 5. Level 5 self-driving cars can be driven entirely by the AI and without any human driver needed. Indeed, for a Level 5 there is usually no pedals and no steering wheel since the expectation is that there won't be a human driver and therefore no need to provide such controls. Self-driving cars that are less-than a Level 5 are considered co-sharing of the driving task, doing so with the AI and the human driver. A human driver must be present and ready to drive for a self-driving car less than a Level 5.

Tesla's cars are considered currently as around a Level 2 or Level 3. As reported in the news, some Tesla owners have from time-to-time claimed that their cars did strange things such as the doors of the car opting to unlock by themselves. This would be disconcerting since if you've parked your car someplace and are in say the grocery store, you'd be worried that your car might suddenly unlock itself and perhaps be vulnerable to hoodlums or being stolen. There are reports that allegedly sometimes a car will open the door while the car is in motion. Again, this is problematic and quite dangerous, if true.

For conventional cars, when a ghost occurs, it is almost always about some mechanical or physical item that perhaps is wearing out or defective or is broken. When an AI self-driving car has a ghost, it could be that the software has inadvertently caused a problem to appear. Suppose the AI system gets into a part of the code that has to do with unlocking the car, and due to perhaps the code being improperly written, it opts to unlock the car even though there's no sound basis to do so at that moment in time. Same could occur with opening the car door.

If the AI developer did not anticipate the car door possibly opening while the car is in motion, they might not have developed the code to try and prevent opening the car door while the car is in motion. It could be that the developer did not write anything that would intentionally open the door while it is in motion, and therefore the developer makes the assumption that it won't ever happen. But, it could be that something else invokes the car door opening code and violates the assumption that the developer made. Without having anticipated that the car door might open while the car is motion, the developer didn't even put in place any kind of double-check in the code to prevent this from happening.

Some pundits for AI self-driving cars are of the belief that the AI will be so good that it would somehow magically "know" to not open the car door when the car is in motion. These pundits seem to believe that the AI will have the same kind of "common sense reasoning" that humans have. There is still much debate by the AI community about whether common sense reasoning is needed for AI self-driving cars. I'll say right now that we're not going to have common sense reasoning for at least the first generation of true AI self-driving cars, so don't be betting that this notion of "common sense" will exist in and be watching over your self-driving car for you.

Where might ghosts surface in an AI self-driving car? Let's consider the key aspects for an AI self-driving car, which consist of:

- Sensor data collection and interpretation
- Sensor fusion
- Virtual world model updating
- AI action planning
- Car controls command issuance

There can be a potential ghost appearance in any of those key areas. A ghost frequency can be:

- Occur just once and never seemingly appear again
- Occur more than once and seem to occur randomly
- Occur more than once and with a semi-random pattern
- Occur more than once with a determinable pattern

We also need to realize that it might be not just one ghost. Often, one anomaly might occur, and it can spark or generate that another ghost might occur. Someone might believe that there's just one ghost that accounts for all of the ghosting. This though is something that a versed ghostbuster knows to look for. Trying to ascribe mysterious behavior to one ghost might not make sense and it might indeed be more than one that have appeared, and for which they might or might not be related to each other.

Thus, keep these in mind:

- There can be just one ghost

- There can be more than one ghost

- Multiple ghosts might be related to each other

- Multiple ghosts might be unrelated to each other

It's also vital to consider whether the ghost is something relatively benign or whether it can have severe consequences. A ghost that messes with the steering of the AI self-driving car could cause the self-driving car to swerve at the worst of times, perhaps hitting another car or going head-on into a wall. A ghost that causes the headlights to go into high beams, well, certainly annoying, but not a significant safety issue per se (that being said, I'd still want to find the ghost).

From a concern perspective, be looking for:

- The ghost has no adverse consequences and is inconsequential

- The ghost has mild adverse consequences but not substantively unsafe

- The ghost has adverse consequences and is considered mildly unsafe

- The ghost has adverse consequences and is considered unsafe

Let's now walk through an example of a potential ghost in an AI self-driving car and let you be the ghostbuster.

The AI self-driving car is driving along on an open highway and there's no traffic nearby. There's a human occupant in the self-driving car. It's a Level 5 self-driving car and the human is not driving and has no provision to drive the car. The self-driving car is in the slow lane. The self-driving car makes a lane change into the fast lane. It stays in the fast lane for just a brief moment and then changes lanes back into the slow lane.

The human occupant notices the lane change aspects and looks around to see what might have prompted the lane change. There weren't any other cars nearby and it seems mysterious that the AI suddenly decided to change lanes and change back to the lane it was in. One would assume that after getting into the fast lane, the self-driving car would have stayed there for some length of time, otherwise why make the lane change. The human occupant worries that this might be some kind of glitch and wonders if it might happen again, and if so whether it could lead to something bad occurring due to possibly in the future making a mysterious lane change when other cars are nearby and might get hit or perhaps actually hit those other cars.

You get contacted by the human occupant and are told about this seeming ghost. What do you think?

First, let's assume that this "actually happened" in that the human occupant didn't make it up (suppose the human was drunk at the time and just imagined that it occurred). Good news so far is that no one got hurt. It also wasn't a panic move by the self-driving car, such as if the human had reported that the self-driving car swerved wildly. The human also indicated that this is the only time it has happened and that the human has been in this AI self-driving car many times before. It seems to be a one-time ghost. We'd also want to find out if the human had been in the AI self-driving car in a similar circumstance before, namely that there wasn't any nearby traffic and the car was zooming along at high speeds.

So, let's go ahead and try to find the ghost.

With an AI self-driving car, there's a chance that the sensor data might have been recorded either on-board the car or it might have been shared up into the cloud associated with the AI self-driving car. It would be handy to check and see if there might be a recorded indication of what the self-driving car was doing during the time that the reported ghost occurred. Using various specialized system tools, it might be possible to interrogate the recorded data and see if indeed the lane change happened.

One "reasonable" basis for the lane change and then the quick lance change reversal action could be that the AI had detected something in the roadway such as debris. The human occupant might not have seen the debris, or by the time the human looked around the self-driving car might be past the debris thus the human didn't notice it. The AI might have wanted to get into the fast lane, made the move, and then got close to some debris up ahead that was now in the range of the sensors, and opted to switch back into the slow lane to avoid the debris.

I've mentioned many times that once AI self-driving cars become prevalent, the odds are that the human occupants are going to want the AI to explain why it is doing things. In this case of the lane change, it would have been helpful if the AI had let the human know that it was making a lane change reversal due to the debris. This would have reassured the human occupant about what otherwise would seem to be a mystery move. Few of the auto makers and tech firms are working on this kind of explanation capability. Some argue that it would only confuse human occupants and possibly even scare the human occupants. My view is that why not let the human occupants decide whether to turn on or not the explanation capability.

There's another handy reason for the explanation capability, namely that it would provide a kind of audit trail of the behavior of the AI. This could be very handy in situations such as this one of trying to ferret out why the AI opted to make the lane change maneuvers. Some are worried that the explanation capability might be used in lawsuits involving AI self-driving cars, which, actually could be seen as a positive aspect to aid the resolving of lawsuits rather than considering it a negative only.

From a technical perspective, some say this is a hard thing to do, and so they push it off as an "edge" problem for now and something to be dealt with later on. Admittedly, there are explanation aspects that will be hard to turn into any kind of human understandable logical explanation. Suppose the self-driving car is using artificial neural networks and other machine learning systems. Those systems often are not based on a human-understandable logic per se and are instead mathematically based. Yes, it might be tough, but this doesn't necessarily mean impossible to do.

In any case, returning to the case of the ghost that caused the unexpected lane change reversal, let's assume that there was recorded data and upon inspecting the video of the cameras and the radar sensor data, we can ascertain that there was debris in the fast lane and that the self-driving car therefore made a sensible lane change reversal. Happy day, the ghost wasn't a ghost.

Suppose though that there wasn't any debris indicated by any of the sensors. This now means we do indeed have a mystery. The next aspect would be to look at what the sensor fusion did. It might have somehow garbled together the sensor data and inadvertently turned on a flag that said debris is in the roadway. This could be an error in the sensor fusion code. If the sensor fusion passed along the flag to the virtual world model, the virtual world would be marked with an indication of debris in the roadway ahead. Then, during the AI action plan updating, the AI planning portion would believe that there was debris up ahead and possibly opted to invoke a lane change. The lane change commands then would be issued by the car controls commands issuance software.

As you now likely realize, there's a lot of detective work in trying to find the ghost. Given what we've been told about the appearance of the ghost, we'd do a step-by-step way walk through of each of the components of the AI self-driving car to try and ascertain what might have produced the odd behavior. What makes this harder than it seems is that whomever is acting as the detective might not have a means to dig into the AI system to figure things out. Or, there might not be much recorded data about what happened and so there is sparse information available to help solve the mystery.

For those of you with finely honed debugging kinds of skills, you presumably recognize these ghostbuster moves. There's a famous acronym in the computer field known as GIGO, meaning Garbage In Garbage Out. This suggests that if a computer system lets in bad data, it's output is going to be bad too. A more modern version is GDGI, which is Garbage Doesn't Get In, meaning that it is best to design and develop computer systems that prevent garbage from getting in altogether.

In terms of ghosts, if the auto maker or tech firm is focused on Ghosts Don't Get In (GDGI), they are developing their AI systems to try and not only prevent ghosts, but also self-detect ghosts. It is crucial that a true AI self-driving be self-aware to the degree that it can try to detect when it performs oddball behavior. This then can be either self-repaired or at least be reported to the auto maker or tech firm so that they can potentially proactively try to find a remedy, if relevant and needed, and then push it out to the AI self-driving cars before it becomes a prevalent problem.

Ghosts are going to be perceived as being in AI self-driving cars and it's up to the auto makers and tech firms to be ready for it. Too many ghosts could scare the public about the veracity of AI self-driving cars. And, I wouldn't blame the public. AI developers have to think about being ghostbusters, doing so when the AI systems are being developed and also for when the AI systems are in the field and ghost finding and ghost removal are needed in the real-world. That's no apparition.

CHAPTER 4
PUBLIC SHAMING OF
AI SELF-DRIVING CARS

CHAPTER 4

PUBLIC SHAMING OF
AI SELF-DRIVING CARS

You've probably seen a pillory and didn't know that it was called a pillory. A pillory is a device typically made of wood that a person would put their head and hands through three holes and be locked into the hinged wooden block to essentially be put on display. This was usually done in a public square for purposes of shaming a person. Some might call them blocks, though technically this is actually a pillory.

The overall societal notion was to force a person to be in the public eye and allow the public to see the person and know that they were being shamed. Public humiliation would presumably cause the person to realize they had done something wrong and they would want to avoid being publicly humiliated again, thus they would no longer undertake whatever transgression got them into the pillory to begin with.

At times, the pillory was placed up on a raised platform to make the shaming more prominent. These pillories would be setup wherever people might have a good chance of seeing the person, such as in the town square or at a key crossroads leading into town. A description of the crime that the person presumably committed was often listed on a sign nearby the pillory. In case you've never perchance been locked into a pillory, it is generally physical uncomfortable, and so it is both a mental shaming and a physically undesirable situation too. Usually the subject in the pillory would only need to be there for a few hours.

Whenever someone was confined to the pillory, word would often quickly spread and people would go out of their way to come and see who was in it and also seek to taunt the person. Thus, it wasn't just that whomever wandered by the pillory would happen to see the person, it was actually a kind of notable event that would attract attention. This was an added "bonus" for those attempting to shame the person, since if otherwise no one actually came to see the offender, it would not make perhaps as dramatic an impression on that offending person and have the justice impact intended. In some cases, the audience would mock the person and even throw items at them, such as rotted fruit or worse still excrement from say a horse or other animal.

At times, the crowd would get rowdy and go overboard in terms of the foul treatment toward the person in the pillory. Officials would at times turn a blind eye to this behavior and let it happen, figuring that they weren't meting out that kind of punishment and it was instead the wisdom of the crowd. If the crowd did harm the person, it would send a signal to warn others that getting into the pillory could have very adverse consequences. Sometimes, officials would overtly and intentionally provide rough treatment. The person's hair might be cut off, they might be whipped, they might be burned or scared, etc. In some instances, they might have a finger cutoff or other body maiming might take place.

On a rare occasion, the crowd might actually be sympathetic towards the person in the pillory. Perhaps the public thought the person was innocent of the claimed transgression. Or, maybe the person committed the transgression but the people believed it be done accidentally or that the pillory was excessive punishment for the crime committed. In any case, the crowd might try to help the person to be more comfortable, providing water or shade. The crowd might protect the person from others that wanted to toss things at the person or otherwise shame them. The crowd might even toss flowers or at least put flowers next to the pillory to send a signal that they did not believe the person deserved the punishment. It could be that the person was a town hero that maybe politically was out of favor of the town officials but that the public at large supported.

You might be thinking that this whole aspect of the pillory is just history. Nobody does this anymore, you might be saying. It's barbaric and we'd not do something like that anymore, you insist.

You are right to the degree that in today's world we have other ways to shame people. The version of the pillory today is often found via the use of social media.

Social media has become a popular and effective modern-day pillory.

Without much cost and effort, you can put someone into a kind of virtual pillory. Make a meme that is catchy and it will go viral. Post something untoward about someone on your blog, and it might get a million hits. Put together a short video clip shaming the person, and it could become a big draw on YouTube. It's easy to do. And, whereas in the past the pillory would only allow a town's worth of people to participate in the shaming, you nowadays can have thousands upon thousands of people from all around the globe that can add to the shaming.

Admittedly, the person isn't confined to the wood blocks and so they aren't forced to sit there and take it. On the other hand, the continual drumming across all of social media can be just as mentally shaming as was the pillory. Think too that half of the planet is involved in shaming you, and it can be pretty damaging to your psyche and ego. The pace at which the public shaming can happen, and the aspect of its geographical spread, across countries, across languages, across cultures, it can be a harsh punishment for someone caught up in it.

At times, the online virtual pillory can become physical and real-world. A person shamed on social media might find themselves being confronted when they try to go and eat in a restaurant. Other patrons might yell at them or threaten them. The restaurant might refuse to feed them a meal. The person can be "shamed" in all areas of life, when eating at a restaurant, when in an airport waiting for a flight, when walking down the street, when sitting in a park, etc. Thus, the social media is more than merely a mental punishment for the person and can have true physical consequences.

Consider too the reputational damage that can be done. The person punished in the old fashioned pillory might have been able to move to a new town and start their life over. Others that they encounter might not have known about the prior pillory experience. With today's social media, the odds are that the virtual pillory will spread far and wide, and the person will be judged everywhere. It also isn't going to readily go away, in that the normal pillory is something that happens for a few hours and it's over, while with social media the virtual pillory might last for years on end (or forever!).

What does the pillory have to do with AI self-driving cars?

At the Cybernetic AI Self-Driving Car Institute, we are developing AI software for self-driving cars, and we also keep up with the latest trends related to AI and to self-driving cars.

One prediction I'll make right now is that we will soon see the AI self-driving car being placed into the virtual pillory on social media.

Allow me a moment to explain.

Right now, AI self-driving cars are just starting to gain some popularity. We're slowly seeing AI self-driving cars becoming used on our public roadways. Until now, self-driving cars were on our roads as a kind of research and development effort. The auto makers and tech firms were using time on the public roads to try and figure out how to code the AI self-driving car to work in the real-world. At some point, the auto makers and tech firms are each deciding it's time to put their self-driving car into use, such as ridesharing for the public, or perhaps as a means to deliver groceries or pizza to a customer that has bought their groceries online or ordered a pizza online or via phone.

Let's clarify what it means to refer to an AI self-driving car. There are various levels of AI self-driving cars. The topmost level is considered Level 5. A Level 5 self-driving car is one that has the AI doing all the driving. For a Level 5, there isn't a human driver. There isn't even usually any provision for a human driver (no pedals, no steering wheel, etc.). The notion is that the AI is supposed to be able to drive the car, doing so like a human could, and not need to rely upon a human for any of the driving. Self-driving cars less-than Level 5 are considered cars that require a human driver, such that the AI and the human driver co-share the driving task. There are dangers associated with the less-than Level 5 self-driving cars as to the co-sharing aspects and confusion that can arise.

With the AI self-driving cars that are less than Level 5, when those self-driving cars get into an accident of some kind, the odds are that the finger will be pointed at the human driver that was supposed to be responsible for the behavior of the car. The auto makers and tech firms certainly prefer to point the finger at the human driver. This absolves the auto maker or tech firm for any blame in the accident, or so they hope it does. This is something still to be ascertained. There are chances that the attempt to shift the attention to the human driver might not work in all cases, and we'll eventually see court cases wherein the human driver is considered perhaps partially at fault and the AI system considered also partially at fault.

Some are worried that if the auto makers and tech firms get pinned with lawsuits that are costly and lead to their AI being considered partially at fault, they'll become the cash cow that the lawsuits will all go after. If this happens, it could dampen the efforts to create AI self-driving cars. Auto makers and tech firms might step back from their efforts under concern of large payouts for lawsuits. Other though say that this is perhaps an appropriate marketplace control on the auto makers and tech firms, forcing those firms to make sure that their AI self-driving cars are sufficiently safe. If they can put self-driving cars onto our roadways that aren't safe and they can just pin the responsibility to the human driver, presumably there's not much teeth in stopping them from generating these unsafe vehicles.

For the true AI self-driving car at a Level 5, there's no means to pin an accident on a human driver in the self-driving car because there isn't one needed in there. Thus, the auto maker or tech firm is potentially exposed. Now, if the AI self-driving car gets into an accident with a conventional car or a less-than Level 5 self-driving car, there's the chance of claiming that the other car caused the accident and the finger can again be pointed to the human driver in that other car. But, otherwise, the AI self-driving car itself will get the spotlight of why it got into an accident.

The regular news media has been very excited about covering AI self-driving car stories. Most of the time, the story is one of wonderment. AI self-driving cars are going to change society and offer many tremendous benefits. News media likes to tout this. The public at large is also eager to see the advent of AI self-driving cars. The public wants to know what's going on. The news media wants to let them know.

This intense interest will tend to magnify anything notable about AI self-driving cars. Sometimes a small story about some "breakthrough" in AI self-driving cars gets star treatment by the news media, even though it's not really much of a genuine breakthrough. On the other side of the coin, when an AI self-driving car gets into an accident, it can also gain headlines. Love or hate, that's the way to get news that will garner eyeballs and attention.

I'm predicting that we'll soon be reaching a stage of evolution of AI self-driving cars in the public eye that will lead to public shaming. The AI self-driving car will be placed into the online virtual pillory.

When an AI self-driving car gets into an accident, particularly a Level 5, it will generate intense focus. If the public believes that the Level 5 self-driving car was out-of-hand, there's a chance of a backlash against AI self-driving cars. If the auto maker or tech firm is not ready to handle the crisis management aspects, they'll likely inadvertently contribute to the public shaming that will arise. Suppose for example that the auto maker or tech firm seems to be stonewalling as to why the AI self-driving car did what it did, this could spark public outrage.

We're used to police today wearing body cams and when a shooting occurs, there is public demands for the video. Some police departments won't release the video, or will only release it once an initial investigation has occurred. The news and the public often don't want to wait. They want to know right away what happened. Holding back the video is a sure way to get their ire. The police often say that the video can be misleading and they want time to figure out what actually happened. The news and the public though often see this as an excuse to not show what's there, and even worse that it maybe implies the police were in the wrong and a cover-up is taking place.

This is quite the same for AI self-driving cars. Everyone knows that an AI self-driving car has cameras, radar, sonar, and other such sensory devices. The moment an accident occurs, the news and the public will be expecting to see a release of the video and any other sensory data, doing so that we can all judge as to what actually happened. The odds are that the auto maker or tech firm will try to respond as the police departments have, namely saying that time is needed to first review the sensor data and that at some future point it will be released. The news and the public aren't likely going to be willing to go along with this notion. They'll assume that stonewalling is taking place, or worse.

If the public gets enraged, you can bet the virtual pillory will go into high gear. Social media will be flooded with public shaming. It will be a vicious cycle of some public shaming that no one notices, and other public shaming that seems to hit a chord and others will re-tweet it or otherwise share it with others. The clever meme's and clever posts will be super-viral.

The ire might be aimed at AI self-driving cars overall. This is bound to be reflected in stock prices of auto makers and tech firms that make AI self-driving cars, namely their stock price will drop precipitously. If the public shaming is large enough, regulators might get activated and try to introduce new legislation that will be onerous on AI self-driving cars. The whole thing can become a cascading mess of a loss of faith in AI self-driving cars.

There's a chance that the public shaming might be aimed at a specific auto maker or tech firm. In that case, the fallout among all AI self-driving car companies might be somewhat lessened. The main brunt might harm that particular firm that was involved in the accident occurring AI self-driving car. It could force that firm to retreat from their AI self-driving car quest. They might need to freeze their further roadway use. They might even stop their internal development efforts. It could cause the firm to go into a "find the witch" mode of self-discovery. And, if there are lawsuits, the firm will need to devote much of its resources to defending the lawsuit, which could detract from any further attempts at moving forward on their AI self-driving car efforts.

The public shaming bandwagon of AI self-driving cars might be powerful enough that it becomes nearly unstoppable. Rather than having just a momentary impact, such as for a day or a week, it could become more permanent and dominant.

Some are worried that it would slow down innovations for AI self-driving cars. It might create such a stigma that AI developers refuse to get associated with an AI self-driving car effort. They might leave those efforts, seeking to apply their AI skills to something else such as for spacecraft, for airplanes, or the like.

As mentioned earlier, the pillory can have momentary impacts or longer term impacts. For a human in a pillory, getting their hand cutoff or being physically scared can last for life. For AI self-driving car companies that get into the virtual pillory, it could either mean just some bad press, of a momentary nature, or it could lead to a widespread and ongoing pillaring of the firm.

There's even a chance that it could put them out of business. They might need to close down entirely their AI self-driving car efforts.

Perhaps they can save whatever else the firm does, though the tainting of their brand might have untoward impacts on the other parts of their enterprise.

AI self-driving cars need to be getting ready for the virtual pillory. They should put in place appropriate crisis management capabilities.

Of course, they should also be designing, developing, and fielding their AI self-driving cars in a sensible manner. If they are skirting the right kinds of protocols and safety measures, the public shaming will not only likely occur, it is likely to be well warranted. Some people historically in the pillory deserved to be there, presumably most deserved it.

With social media, it's at times not so clear that someone placed into the virtual pillory really deserved the full extent of the punishment. Nonetheless, it's todays rapid fire way to do a public shaming. Let's try to avoid the public shaming of AI self-driving cars. Aim instead at public revelation of AI self-driving cars. Maybe flowers will be tossed at us the next time that an AI self-driving car saves a life.

CHAPTER 5
INTERNET OF THINGS (IOT) AND AI SELF-DRIVING CARS

CHAPTER 5

INTERNET OF THINGS (IOT) AND AI SELF-DRIVING CARS

Internet of Things (IoT), it's here already to some extent, it's all around us, and yet it also has only just begun. Some estimates are that there exist today around 8 to 9 billion IoT devices globally, and by the year 2020 there will be perhaps 30 billion IoT devices worldwide. That's a tripling of growth. Some would say that's actually a quite conservative number and the growth could be several times higher.

Where are these IoT devices?

Allow a moment of a brief story to highlight that they are in places that we don't yet traditionally think they would be.

Recently, during an internationally televised news conference, the President of Russia handed a soccer ball to the President of the United States, doing so as a result of the world soccer games that were held in Russia and with similar games to occur in the U.S. in the future. This seemed at the moment like a gracious act, a light-hearted matter, and something that added a sunnier touch to the otherwise very heavy and dark matters that the two heads of state would normally be consumed with (small things like nuclear weapons!).

A news agency later on pointed out that the soccer ball might have an IoT device in it. Heavens! Was this a Cold War era kind of trick to get the President of the United States to carry around a secret listening device wherever he might go? Just imagine this soccer ball traveling with him on Air Force One, capturing the most private of conversations. Imagine the soccer ball sitting on his desk in the White House. There it is, in plain sight, and yet no one suspecting that it's transmitting tons of American secrets straight back to the Kremlin.

Well, of course it had an IoT device in it. Many of the latest soccer balls have a computer chip that is used to transmit information to a mobile app or similar system and indicate how many times the ball is kicked, how fast it goes, and the like. In this case, it was an Adidas soccer ball and openly advertised that it has a chip, along with there being a tag on the outside of the soccer ball to indicate that it contained a chip.

Admittedly, most people aren't yet familiar with chips inside soccer balls, baseballs, footballs, basketballs, and the like. In some cases, the costs of adding the chip have kept those sporting goods items at a higher price point and so not yet found their way into the hands of the masses. In other cases, people aren't yet comfortable with their sporting goods being able to record and communicate, and likely until the existing generation becomes adults will we see widespread acceptance (i.e., the kids of today, upon becoming adults in the future, will want such features and fully expect that all sporting goods items will have them built-in).

So, there were many of us in the high-tech field that were bemused at this outcry of a "transmitter" being inside the soccer ball. Yes, we said, there's a chip in there and what's new news about that? To keep the story going, the conspiracy theorists said that the Russians knew that we knew that a soccer ball would have a chip in it, and so they Russians hacked it or replaced it with a true tracking device, and figured we'd not notice because we would assume it was only a conventional soccer ball containing a conventional computer chip. The old switcheroo.

Or, maybe we knew that they knew that we knew, and so maybe the President has been whispering things to the soccer ball that are faked secrets, in hopes that the Russians will believe it. Now that makes the most sense for sure!

Anyway, the point of the story is that we are gradually seeing that IoT devices are everywhere around us. Indeed, some claim that on a daily basis we might have 1,000 to 5,000 objects surrounding us at any point in time that could potentially someday have an IoT device on them. We are headed toward an era known as ubiquitous computing or what some call pervasive computing. This refers to computers that are everywhere we are.

What has suddenly brought forth this emergence of IoT? It's the grand convergence of the ongoing miniaturization of computers, allowing them to be small enough to put on just about anything. These chips are also durable enough that they can survive while on whatever they are placed on or into. They are powerful enough to have features that make them useful, such as sensing light, sensing temperature, capturing sounds, etc. They are getting lower in cost; thus they are inexpensive to use. Some even say that we should consider this to be "disposable" computing, meaning that it is so cheap that even if only used for short duration and then discarded, it's worth the cost.

As aside, there are concerns that disposable computing is going to become a massive environmental nightmare. Right now, we're all concerned that there are too many plastic straws and plastic bags being tossed into our landfills and oceans. Think about how much ecological damage those millions upon millions of discarded computer chips could create. But, that's a different topic. Let's get back to the topic at-hand.

What really makes these IoT devices significant is that they have the ability to electronically communicate. If they were simply standalone non-connectable devices that couldn't tattle, we all probably would not be so excited about them. These though have the ability to electronically communicate to the outside world. That's the "Internet" part of the Internet of Things mantra. These devices can connect with something else, typically via WiFi or Bluetooth or NFC or whatever, and what they have to say can quickly go around the world.

The advent of IoT is going to likely have profound impacts on society. Imagine computer chips on our clothing ala FitBit, and imagine computer chips on all of your items at home such as your refrigerator and coffee maker, and computer chips on your items at the office such as your chairs and stapler, etc. All of these chips being able to have some kind of sensory capability. All of these chips having an ability to electronic communicate whatever they detect. The "dumb" objects around us will all become "smart" objects by the addition of IoT. If the object itself gets feedback from the chip, and can adjust based on the feedback, the object itself then becomes possibly "personalized" in a manner that otherwise it was just a mass commodity item.

With great promise there is often great peril. The privacy ramifications are enormous. It will be like having eyes and ears being able to detect our every move. It will be electronically communicated, perhaps without you even knowing that it has. The data then might be used in very untoward and at times scary ways.

There's the security aspects that also give us all grey hair. You probably are aware that there are thousands of baby cams that people put in their home nursery so they could watch their baby while at work or in another room of their house. Turns out that many of those IoT devices had a default password that people didn't change when they setup the baby cam. All of a sudden, nefarious people tapped into these baby cams and posted them onto the Internet. Some of these posts were done to showcase how "stupid" people were about their security. Others posted it out of other less noble reasons.

So, we will get home automation, connected health, wearable tech, and all of these other exciting aspects via IoT, but we also will get the chances of humongous privacy violations and possibly tons upon tons of computer security problems. Life always seems to do things this way.

There's going to be "Enterprise IoT" consisting of IoT in the workplace. There's going to be "Home IoT" consisting of home automation. There's going to be "Individual" IoT, consisting of us wearing or maybe inserting into our bodies all sorts of IoT devices.

What else might there be?

There is going to be "AI Self-Driving Cars" IoT. Yes, Internet of Things will be intersecting with AI self-driving cars. Mark my words!

At the Cybernetic AI Self-Driving Car Institute, we are developing AI systems for self-driving cars. Among the many facets of how high-tech will come to play in self-driving cars, the advent of IoT is absolutely going to be a part of AI self-driving cars.

There are these key ways that IoT will be involved with AI self-driving cars:

- **IoT Self**: AI self-driving car is in a sense, in of itself, a large-scale IoT device

- **IoT Add-ons**: IoT devices natively included into an AI self-driving car

- **IoT Walk-in's**: IoT devices brought into an AI self-driving car usually temporarily

- **IoT Nearby**: IoT devices outside and nearby an AI self-driving car and within communication range

For some, they are either blindly just pretending that IoT is not going to be a factor involving AI self-driving car, or they assume they'll catch-up later on. Better still, look ahead to the future and realize that the AI self-driving car needs to be ready for an IoT world and we should be preparing for that future today. That's what we are doing, getting ready for it.

Few of the auto makers or tech firms are giving this much consideration right now. They would say this is an "edge" problem, meaning that it is not at the core of what is needed to get an AI self-driving car to undertake the driving task. Yes, it could be considered an edge problem, but it's an important one and it should not be ignored or neglected.

Let's consider each of the key ways in which an AI self-driving car is impacted by IoT devices.

The most apparent way involves considering the AI self-driving car as an IoT device. It's connected and can appear to be an IoT. Now, we all know that it's a large-scale IoT and not some simple chip. Nonetheless, from the perspective of someone on the Internet, it could appear like its something that is an IoT. This brings up the myriad of privacy and security concerns about AI self-driving cars.

Next, there are going to be IoT devices natively in an AI self-driving car. Auto makers and tech firms are going to have discussions with various IoT device makers and realize that it would make sense to add those IoT devices into the self-driving car. Rather than the auto maker or tech firm having to do everything regarding the self-driving car, it's going to be more expedient to use other third-party IoT devices.

This can be as straightforward as the entertainment systems in an AI self-driving car, which given that people are likely to be in their self-driving car a lot of the time, it is anticipated that most of the true AI self-driving cars are going to be internally outfitted like your own movie theatre. For that two-hour morning commute, you won't be driving the car, so what else will you do? Watch a movie, or maybe take a course from an online university. The inside of the self-driving car is going to have tons of electronics and most of those are going to be IoT-related devices.

There are some that are even designing IoT devices for the exterior of your self-driving car. Maybe you want to collect some data about the world outside of your AI self-driving car and none of the already built-in sensors will collect it. So, instead, you have included onto the outside body of your self-driving car IoT devices for that purpose. You then collect the electronic data that streams from those devices.

The third aspect of IoT for AI self-driving cars involves bringing IoT devices into the self-driving car. Suppose you are ridesharing and opt to use someone else's AI self-driving car. You meanwhile have a dozen different IoT devices on you, including for your watch, for your jewelry, in your shoes, in your jacket, etc. You are a walking smorgasbord of IoT devices. When you step into that AI self-driving car, they are all going into the self-driving car with you. By-and-large, they will be in the AI self-driving car temporarily, typically for the duration of your ridesharing trip (and, then, you get out of the AI self-driving car, along with the cornucopia of IoT devices already on you).

What difference does it make that you are bringing those dozen or more IoT devices into the AI self-driving car?

Here's some possibilities:

- You might want to connect your IoT devices with the WiFi or other communications capability of the AI self-driving car so that you can get Internet service to your IoT devices.

- You might want your IoT devices to communicate directly to the AI self-driving car.

- You might want to have your IoT devices communicate with the IoT devices already in the AI self-driving car.

- Etc.

There's some bad news right now about these possibilities. The standards and protocols for IoT devices are still somewhat blurry and not well formulated and not well accepted. Things are pretty fragmented right now. This means that you could end-up that many of your walk-in IoT devices aren't going to be readily able to communicate either with the AI self-driving car and nor with the other IoT devices in the AI self-driving car. This is something still needed to be worked out.

Another concern is the swamping factor. You get into the AI self-driving car, and all of sudden it's trying to devote a lot of attention to electronically communicating with your IoT devices. Will this distract from the act of driving the self-driving car? Will it consume limited computing resources available in the self-driving car that otherwise should go toward other tasks?

Add to this the other possibility mentioned of IoT Nearby, which is that there are going to be lots of IoT devices outside of your AI self-driving car, ones that you drive past, ones that when you are parked your self-driving car is near to, and how will your AI self-driving car handle their nearness and attempts to poke and prod? They might all be bombarding your AI self-driving car with requests to electronically communicate. Which of those requests are worthy, and which are not?

Some worry that we'll see the classic DoS (Denial of Service) attack occur at AI self-driving cars. A nefarious person might purposely try to overwhelm your AI self-driving car by beaming thousands of requests from IoT devices sitting by the roadside. This is actually something that is being actively researched and often referred to as DDoS (Distributed Denial of Service).

You might say, well, just have the AI self-driving car deny all requests to communicate. But, suppose we have speed limit signs that are digitally-based and transmit the allowed maximum speed on that stretch of road to your AI self-driving car. Suppose there's a traffic signal up ahead sending out an electronic signal that the light is about to go red. And, there's a bridge over the next hill that is sending out an electronic signal that there's been a car accident on the bridge and to watch out for slowing traffic. These are all legitimate V2I (vehicle to infrastructure) kinds of IoT communications.

I realize that presumably there should be some kind of special encoding that indicates when a legitimate IoT is trying to communicate with your AI self-driving car. Even once we get there, keep in mind that there are bound to be spoofing efforts to mimic those real signals. Plus, suppose that the geographical area you are driving in has thousands of these legitimate V2I going on. It could be that no one thought beforehand about how much the V2I electronic traffic there would be, and the city or locale has just kept adding IoT after IoT, under the assumption that more is better.

Let's also include into this mix something else that is both good and bad about IoT, namely V2V. V2V is vehicle to vehicle communications. The idea is that AI self-driving cars will electronically communicate and share with each other about what's going on. An AI self-driving car that's a mile ahead of you on the freeway might inform your AI that the freeway is blocked. Thus, your AI self-driving car might realize it should get off the freeway at the next exit and use side streets to get around the snarl.

Do you want your AI self-driving car to communicate with any and all other AI self-driving cars that also have V2V? Maybe not. Suppose someone gets their AI to send something untoward or incorrect to your AI self-driving car. Perhaps I'm in traffic behind you, and I want your self-driving car out of my way, so I have my AI self-driving car tell your AI self-driving car that the traffic further up ahead is snarled, and it convinces your AI to get off the freeway. Nice, since I now have a clearer path ahead for my AI self-driving car.

We also need to consider what your V2V is going to tell other self-driving cars about you. Suppose you get into my ridesharing AI self-driving car and your IoT devices that you bring into the AI self-driving car are able to communicate with the AI self-driving car. The AI self-driving car discovers that you are overweight via an IoT device you are wearing for fitness purposes. This is sent via the V2V to another car up ahead that has arranged for an advertiser to use the outside of the self-driving car as an electronic billboard. The ad now displays a new diet regimen that a company is trying to sell, with the ad timed so that as the ridesharing AI self-driving car goes past it, you'll be right there to see the ad.

These IoT devices can communicate with each other in potentially real-time, and rapidly transmit around the electronic information in ways that you might not even consider.

Consider another possible concern. There is likely to be a camera pointed inward in most AI self-driving cars. This allows the owner of the AI self-driving car to see what's going on inside the AI self-driving car, such as if they are renting it out as a ridesharing vehicle. Let's also assume there is an audio capture capability too.

When you get into that AI self-driving car as a rideshare passenger, maybe it videos you. It then beams the video via its own Internet connection, or maybe passes it along to some other IoT device in the AI self-driving car or near to it.

This takes us back to the earlier points about IoT and privacy. Digital surveillance will be ramped up with the advent of IoT. We are going to be surrounded by trackable objects. They will be with us, while walking down the street, and while riding in an AI self-driving car. The AI self-driving car itself is a variant of an IoT, and will contain IoT's, some of which were purposely put there, others that you bring into the self-driving car. Will we need governmental regulation to help protect us? Can government protection even do so? Do we want the government to intervene?

Suppose too that someone gets into an AI self-driving car and secretly plants an IoT device in that ridesharing vehicle?

They hide it under a seat or manage to put it inside the self-driving car so that it looks as though it properly belongs there.

Similar to the soccer ball story, it might now be listening and recording everyone else that comes into that AI self-driving car.

Shocking? Maybe for us, but the next generation that grows-up with pervasive computing and IoT is not going to be particularly surprised by this kind of item. They will have grown-up knowing about it.

Presumably, AI self-driving car makers will even provide some kind of electronic sweeping device that can detect what IoT's are in the self-driving car. Maybe even be able to prevent unauthorized IoT's from functioning. We'll have to see how far this goes.

The rise of IoT is aligned with the rise of AI self-driving cars. It's crucial to anticipate what the intersection of the two will produce. And, it's important the auto makers and tech firms design their AI self-driving cars accordingly. This is one of those technical topics that's also a societal topic that is also a business topic which is also a governmental topic, all rolled into one. IoT and AI self-driving cars, they are a potential match made in heaven. Let's just protect ourselves from the devil and a potential inferno.

.

CHAPTER 6

PERSONAL RAPID TRANSIT (PRT) AND SELF-DRIVING CARS

CHAPTER 6

PERSONAL RAPID TRANSIT (PRT) AND SELF-DRIVING CARS

I've ridden many times on the BART system in San Francisco (that's the Bay Area Rapid Transit, or BART system, which provides mass transit throughout the Bay Area).

Typically, during work transit times in the morning and the evening, each person is sitting (or standing) and trying to carve out their own little world while being jam packed with lots of other people in the sardine can of a train car. Many people are wearing audio headsets to block out the noises around them. Many are wearing sunglasses or something to try and mask their gaze. I've even recently seen some wearing a mobile Virtual Reality (VR) headset, which really does help to block out the real-world and enter into a dreamscape world.

Mass transit for many people is something they'd prefer to not be involved in. Being around lots of other people can be confining. Most people are relatively sane and allow you some privacy, but you've then got the wild passengers that insist on trying to draw attention. They dance, they sing, they make a spectacle. There are some that seek money. There are some that just seem to have lost their wits and are inane as they speak or make sounds or movements. It can be quite a ride.

I know it would seem like a small price to pay for being more economical about the cost of transit. I know too that it is better for the environment to have people transported via a large-scale operation. It presumably drops the pollution per capita of those traveling. It might even reduce the transportation costs per capita, per mile traveled and per person traveling. There is certainly a long list of important reasons to have mass transit.

Though the case is compelling, it goes against our seemingly innate desire to travel with control over our own space. When you are in a mass transit situation, whether being on a bus, a tram, a train, a subway, a commercial plane, etc., you are inevitably forced into being in a large group.

You have no choice. Once you step into the mass transit, you become a member of the mass. You then must be around and immersed within the mass. Some commercial flights provide a bubble berth for First Class passengers that want to sleep and have their own privacy. That's a rarity, though, and most of the time you become a member of the mass.

When you drive your car, you are in a sense "separated" from the mass. You now have your own bubble, as it were. You are within the mass, but you have your own space. You are overall separated from the mass.

Of course, your car will be immersed within the mass, such as when you are on the freeway, but you still have your own space. It's kind of amazing when you think about it – you can be bumper to bumper on the freeway, your car is a scant few inches from cars all around you, and yet you still don't need to interact with the people in those cars, and you are able to create your own internal environment. You set the temperature as you wish, you play music as you wish, you move around in your space as you wish, etc.

One of the reasons that especially Southern California has had such a hard time of getting adoption of mass transit is that no one wants to give up their own separate space. They don't want to give up their own control over their miniature environment in their own bubble. They want to keep their own bubble, and yet have that bubble get them over to work or to the ballgame. I realize it might seem ironic that you'd be willing to sit in a Dodger Stadium with 56,000 other unseparated people, and yet still insist on your own bubble when getting to and going away from the baseball field, but that's what it seems to culturally be.

To be fair, for the purposes of transportation, it's also about wanting to get to where you want to go, doing so when you want to do so. When you use mass transit, you must conform to the schedule for the masses. That BART train leaves from the Powell station at 2:10 p.m. and again at 3:05 p.m., and you need to conform to that schedule. With your own personal transportation, you decide when you want to leave. Maybe it's 2:20 p.m., and you decide it's time to go, well, you jump into your car and away you go.

There are mass transit pundits that will counter argue that you might indeed be able to leave when you want via your own personal transportation, but it doesn't mean you'll arrive when you want. In other words, the BART train might get to your desired location at 4:00 p.m. by having left at 2:10 p.m., meanwhile if you leave in your car at 2:20 p.m. you might not get to your destination until 5:00 p.m. Thus, you might be fooled or lulled into believing you are controlling your transportation, but you would actually be more efficient if you used the mass transit.

We can go back-and-forth about this. In the end, most people do not opt to use mass transit.

We'll for the moment agree that it is due to the ability to have unscheduled times of transportation, and be able to travel in small groups of your own choosing and have a controlled bubble when doing so. Whether this is selfish is another matter. Whether people are right or wrong as to what they choose to do, as based on some viewpoint of societal good, that's again another matter too. I'm not going to get overly fixated here on a lengthy debate about the efficacy of mass transit in society.

Let's instead discuss something related to mass transit, namely Personal Rapid Transit (PRT).

You might not be familiar with PRT. There aren't many PRT's in existence. There has been a fair amount of discussion and research about PRT's. You've likely "seen" a PRT as portrayed in a science fiction movie or comic books. Unlikely that you've ridden in a real-world one.

The concept is that you would be able to leverage some aspects of mass transit, but then have some aspects of personal transit. You might view this as being the best of two worlds. There are others that would say that you actually end-up with the worst of two worlds.

Usually, a PRT consists of some kind of pods, often referred to as podcars. These podcars allow you to have your own separate space, though they usually consist of seating for maybe 3 to 6 people. We'll call that a small group.

The podcar looks somewhat like one of those airport trams you've probably taken, though think of it as just one train car and much smaller in size so that it seats a handful of people at most. For those of you that used to visit Disneyland in the olden days, they had the People Mover which had what might be called podcars (and it didn't even take an E ticket to ride one!). For some ski resorts, they have a tramway that is small enough that you could consider it to be about the same as a podcar.

So, the podcar provides the first part of the equation, an ability to have your own bubble (pretty much). The second part of the equation is the unscheduled times to get to where you want to go. Let's consider how that works.

The PRT is supposed to consist of a network of special guideways, upon which the podcars operate. The topology of the network allows for the podcars to proceed across the network and not need to stop at intermediary locations. Imagine if we had a network grid, let's say like a spreadsheet shape, and we'll call the columns by letters of the alphabet and the rows by numbers.

You get into a podcar at position A1. You want to get to position B5 on the network grid. With a typical mass transit system, the train car at A1 might stop at A2, then A3, then A4, then A5, and then proceed to B5. You've made a series of stops to get to your destination. A podcar of a PRT would be intended to go from A1 to B5 without any intermediary stops. It would pass through A2, A3, A4, A5, and then arrive to B5.

Thus, you get your own space and which leaves when you want and goes directly to where you want.

Kind of.

How do you know that a podcar will be waiting for you at A1 when you arrive? Answer, there are either lots of podcars all throughout the network and one is always ready to go, or, instead, you bring your own podcar. Keep this in mind for a moment and I'll further elaborate shortly.

How do you know that the podcar will go straight to B5 without stopping in-between? That's up to the system that coordinates the movement of the podcars. It is typically a centralized control of the podcars and the system is trying to ensure you don't stop. Of course, this is not as easy as it seems, since it depends upon the other traffic on the network and the overall capacity and availability of the network. In some cases, the podcars might also operate by peer-to-peer coordination, rather than a centralized control.

The goal of a PRT is to have personal oriented rapid transit, doing so to overcome the qualms people have about using mass transit. Proponents of PRT would say that it also can be done at a lower construction cost than MRT (Mass Rapid Transit), and with less regulatory easements needed, and be less obtrusive, and so on. And would have greater acceptance by society. The PRT is built with the guideways and network being protected so that it can whisk along the podcars at very high speeds.

Opponents of PRT say it's a boondoggle that in the end won't approach the lesser costs of MRT and the lessened environmental advantages, and that the money spent on PRT is tossing good money after bad. The MRT proponents would say that the PRT money should be spent instead on MRT, and that PRT is an unfortunate distraction and drain away from the focus that should be on MRT.

I have no dog in this fight right now about the PRT versus MRT battle herein. If you are intrigued by the debate, go find a proponent of PRT and a proponent of MRT, and let them go at each other.

Meanwhile, here's what I'd like to cover.

What does all of this have to do with AI self-driving cars?

At the Cybernetic AI Self-Driving Car Institute, we are developing AI systems for self-driving cars. We are also exploring innovative offshoots of AI self-driving cars. PRT is one such offshoot.

Remember that I earlier said that the podcar waiting for you at position A1 of the PRT network might be a podcar pre-arranged there for use, or it might be that you bring your own podcar. Some PRT designers have pointed out that maybe there's not a need to have lots of standing by podcars in a PRT. Instead, if someone drivers their own car, why not turn it into a podcar, so to speak.

Here's how it would work.

You drive up on your car to a podcar station. You drive your car into a kind of shell. Your car is now inside this shell. You stop driving your car at this juncture. The wheels of the car are locked into place inside the shell. You've maybe done something like this when you went to a car wash. At some car washes, you drive up to the entrance, you turn off your engine, you've positioned the car into special wheel wells, and now a conveyor belt pulls or pushes along your car through the car wash. Same concept for the PRT, except sorry, your car isn't going to get washed while in the PRT (but, hey, that's another idea!).

Your car now is your personal space and it is in the shell (in essence, your car inside the shell is now in totality a podcar, for the moment). The shell moves along within the network of the PRT. When you arrive at the destination, say position B5, the shell opens up and you drive out. You've done the same thing likely on ferries that cross a river or body of water.

Suppose you don't have a car? Will this PRT be only for those that happen to have a car? If so, it seems like an elitist form of transit because a person has to be able to afford a car. Answer, there will be podcars that are available in case you don't have a car. The good news is that you presumably won't need so many of these podcars because by-and-large most people are going to be using their cars instead.

Now, I'll clarify, not all PRT's are designed the same way, and thus there indeed might be a PRT that requires you must have a car and there aren't any podcars available per se. There are other PRT's that don't make use of cars at all and require that you only ride in the specially prepared podcars. Just wanted to clarify.

Could an AI self-driving car ride on a PRT?

Sure.

If you consider for the moment that a car simply drives into a shell and then parks, it would be hoped that any AI self-driving car could do this. There are various levels of self-driving cars. A Level 5 is a true self-driving car, which is one that is driven entirely by the AI and there isn't any human driver involved. Cars less than a Level 5 are intended to be driven by both a human driver and the AI, doing so in a co-sharing manner. There must be a human driver present in the less than Level 5's and the human driver must be ready to take over the car controls.

I think we can all agree that any AI self-driving car, regardless of the level, would or certainly should be able to drive into the shell and park. This seems like an easy task, either for the AI or for the co-sharing human driver in the case of cars less than Level 5. No big deal here.

We would certainly expect too that the AI self-driving car can drive into the shell, park, and then when the shell gets whisked to its destination, the AI could drive the self-driving car out of the shell and go on its presumably merry way. Easy peasy.

One mild concern is whether the self-driving car will fit inside the shell. This is of course a question that needs to be asked about any car, even a conventional car. The shells won't necessarily accommodate any size car. Also, a car that has ski racks on the top and looks like it is outfitted to go in a parade, it might also not fit. Generally, since most of the AI self-driving cars are based on the frame and structure of a conventional car, and even if it has a LIDAR unit on the top of the self-driving car, it would be reasonable to think it will fit into the shell.

The more interesting question is what will the AI self-driving car be doing while inside the shell and serving as the personal space ala podcar?

You could decide that the AI self-driving car is doing nothing particular special while sitting inside the shell. It is no different than a conventional car at this point. It's just a receptacle that is parked inside the shell and (possibly) has people inside of it (note that it doesn't necessarily have human occupants, as it could be that as an AI self-driving car it has driven itself to the PRT and it is merely wanting to use the PRT to get to some other part of town).

The AI self-driving car at this juncture inside the PRT could be considered a "dumb" car as it no longer is doing anything active. It's simply along for the ride, as it were.

Another perspective is that maybe we use the AI smarts as part of the PRT system. Perhaps the PRT system taps into the AI of the self-driving cars that are in the PRT, and uses them to help coordinate the movement of the podcars. In fact, since AI self-driving cars are intended to likely have V2V (vehicle to vehicle communication), it could be that the AI self-driving cars all operate within the PRT to do a peer-to-peer coordination of the movement of the podcars.

This then leverages the otherwise dormant AI and computer processing that is sitting idle while the AI self-driving car is acting like a passenger in the PRT. Any AI self-driving car that wanted to ride the PRT would need to download an app, akin to downloading an app on your mobile phone. Once the app was installed in the AI self-driving car, it could then be an active participant in the PRT. If it did not have the app, it could not be an active participant.

One downside to this approach consists of the aspect that what about conventional cars that might want to also use the PRT? They don't have the computer processing and the AI to actively participate in the PRT transportation coordination. You could say that those conventional cars, or those AI self-driving cars that don't decide to actively participate, are then coordinated by the AI self-driving cars that are participating. Or, maybe a centralized control system then deals with those podcars. It is something that needs to be considered and figured out.

The AI self-driving car could be doing other things while inside the shell, doing something other than non-driving. For most AI self-driving cars, they will need to periodically do OTA (Over The Air) updates, which will usually be undertaken while the AI self-driving car is relatively dormant.

Doing the OTA during the PRT riding might be a convenient time and place, depending upon whether it makes sense to do so (if the OTA will take two hours and the ride time on the PRT is only 15 minutes, probably wise to not start the OTA).

The AI self-driving car could also be interacting with the occupants during the PRT ride time. It is generally assumed that the inside of an AI self-driving car is going to be outfitted with elaborate electronic entertainment options. You are going to be in your self-driving car quite a bit and have no need to be driving, and so the odds are that you'll be doing some kind of game playing or maybe some kind of online educational learning, and so on. All of those aspects can still be underway while you are in the PRT.

In fact, in one sense, the human occupants of the true AI self-driving car might not know or even care that they are inside the PRT system.

Here's why.

Let's pretend you've told your AI self-driving car to get you across town. You leave it up to the AI to decide how to best get there. It calculates that the roadways are jammed. It therefore drives to the nearest pod station of the PRT, gets into a shell, whisks along to the destination, drives out of the shell, and takes you the last mile to your destination. You were the entire time absorbed inside the self-driving car with that exciting class on the philosophy of Aristotle that you are taking during your morning commute, and had no idea that for part of the ride that you happened to end-up in the PRT.

One criticism of PRT's is that it still does not solve the last mile problem. In other words, there are going to be only so many of the podcar stations around town. The stations aren't going to be at every block and intersection. So, you'll still need a means to get to wherever the access points are for using the PRT, doing so from your home or from your office or from the store, etc. The AI self-driving car is one means to get that last mile.

You could use something else, such as a scooter to get there (and then use a PRT provided podcar), but the concept will be that you'd normally use some more robust personal space device like a car or a self-driving car.

Some people say that with PRT, we'd need less cars. We'd need less conventional cars and we'd need less AI self-driving cars. That could be true. That's certainly the intent of the mass transit systems. Presumably, the same should be true of the PRT. Some don't like the idea of the PRT allowing cars as the podcars, because they believe it merely fosters a car culture. They say let's get rid of cars. We need to discourage cars, rather than encouraging them by finding other means to keep them around.

Others believe that the PRT might aid the expanded use of AI self-driving cars. The AI self-driving cars will be routinely going back-and-forth from people's home or work or whatever, and going to the PRT, like bees going to a beehive. There are some that think it will foster more carpooling, since you and I might live next door to each other, but work in different parts of town, but we both get into our jointly owned AI self-driving car (or someone else's ridesharing AI self-driving car), it uses the PRT to get close to my office and then drops me off, and then gets back into the PRT to do the same for you.

It's hard to say whether and to what degree the PRT will discourage or encourage car use, whether conventional car or AI self-driving car.

Is there any chance at all that a PRT like this will even be built and be put into use?

Elon Musk believes so. He recently spoke here in Los Angeles and provided his latest vision of a PRT that he calls the Loop.

You drive your car, hopefully in his case a Tesla, into a shell, doing so at ground level, and an elevator takes it underground. There is an elaborate tunnel system underground that acts as the network of the PRT. Once you reach your destination station, the elevator lifts the car back to ground level and you drive off. He's drafted a map of 60 miles of tunnels with about 23 stops that his Boring company would create here in Southern California.

Critics decried his vision as impractical and unworkable. There will be long lines of cars at the pod stations, all waiting to get into a pod shell.

Cars will be backed up for miles and it will be worse environmentally and disruptive to anyone working or living near a pod station.

The places where the pod stations are located have been criticized as not enough of them and they are at places that seem randomly chosen rather than chosen for purposes of reducing travel time for those living here.

Some said he ought to help improve the mass transit system here, rather than avoiding doing so by concocting something else entirely. And so on.

Maybe his vision needs tweaking.

Or, maybe, like anything that's a first try attempt, it needs more refinement. Or, maybe indeed, as some accuse, it's a wacky idea. No one really knows.

Other attempts at PRT's have been met with resistance, some have met financial ruin, some have been unable to navigate the regulatory approvals, some had engineering design flaws. You name it.

That being said, I don't think that whether or not there are PRT's especially impacts the progress on AI self-driving cars.

I figured you'd be relieved to know that.

I do though consider the PRT to be another interesting "edge" problem for AI self-driving cars, meaning a problem not necessarily core to AI self-driving cars, but one that is nonetheless worthy of attention for AI self-driving cars.

I'll let you know when we get our AI self-driving car to be one of the first to drive on the SoCal PRT and will post pictures of it getting into and out of the pod shells, when or if that day arrives. Meanwhile, we'll all need continue enjoying driving our PNRT's, Personal Non-Rapid Transit conventional cars.

CHAPTER 7

EVENTUAL CONSISTENCY AND AI SELF-DRIVING CARS

CHAPTER 7

EVENTUAL CONSISTENCY
AND AI SELF-DRIVING CARS

Consistency. Maybe so, maybe not. One of the hot topics in the distributed computer systems realm involves notions of consistency. Simple stated, if you have multiple machines that are intended to store some particular data, what are the various ways that you can keep that data "consistent" across those myriad of machines, meaning that the same data is at those machines whenever you opt to take a look.

This is a lot harder to arrange than it might seem at first glance.

Let's use an everyday example to illustrate this theme about consistency.

Pretend that you have a bank account that has $40 in it. You go to an ATM that's in front of a grocery store and use it to find out your current balance. After logging into the ATM, it confirms that you've got $40 in your bank account.

Later that day you go to the bank and deposit $60 more into your bank account, doing so at the ATM at the bank branch. You walk away from the bank and proceed on your merry way. In theory, you now have $100 in your bank account, due to adding $60 to the $40 that was already there. You are rich!

Perhaps the bank has a centralized computer that keeps track of all of the deposits made at all of the ATM's. When you went to the first ATM at the grocery store, it communicated with the centralized system and found out you had $40 in your account, and the ATM then told you so. When you later on went to the ATM at the bank, it dutifully took your added $60 and communicated with the centralized system to tell it so.

Since you are suspicious of banks and all financial institutions, you decide to once again visit the ATM at the grocery store and double-check that the added $60 is really recorded in your bank account. Who knows, maybe the bank has taken your money and used it for a honeymoon trip to Hawaii.

When you login to the ATM at the grocery store, what do you see?

Well, I'm sure you are expecting to see that you have $100 in your account and that the $60 was properly recorded and added to your balance. Otherwise, it would seem like you've been ripped off and somebodies head should roll.

So that you don't get overwrought, let's pretend that indeed the $100 is shown and also the $60 deposit is shown. Great! The ATM would have communicated with the centralized system, the $60 deposit transaction would have been recorded, and the new balance was calculated. All's good.

Suppose though that when using the ATM at the grocery store this second time, it shows you that you still only have $40 in your bank account and there's no indication that you had made the added $60 deposit. Yikes! You are as angry as a hornet. Of course, it could be that the ATM is unable to connect with the centralized system, and therefore all that this ATM knows is what it last knew, namely that you still only have $40 in your account.

The ATM probably should tell you that it cannot connect with the centralized system and so your balance might be considered outdated or "stale" – just so that you'd know that it might not be showing you the latest and greatest amount in your account. But, you know how computers are, maybe no one thought about this happening and so there's no provision to alert you that you aren't seeing the latest that's contained in the centralized system.

Take a step back and let's rethink this scenario. Imagine that there wasn't a centralized system involved at all. Instead, we opted to completely decentralize the banking systems of the bank. Each ATM would be expected to let all of the other ATM's know when someone's bank account has changed. Thus, when you put $60 into the ATM at the bank branch, the ATM there was supposed to then send a message to the other ATM's, such as the one at the grocery store, letting them know that you've added $60 to your bank account.

When you went to the ATM at the grocery store on your second visit, it might or it might not have yet gotten an update from the ATM at the bank branch. If it did get the update, you'd see that you made the $60 deposit and your $100 balance. If it did not yet get the update, it would assume you still just have the $40. Perhaps all of the ATM's are perfectly able to communicate with each other, but it just takes a length of time for the one ATM to communicate to all the others about the latest update.

In a distributed system, it's important to consider the latency aspects, meaning how long will it take for the distributed members to communicate with each other. If I told you that with your chosen bank you'd need to wait at least 24 hours before your updates at the one branch ATM propagated to all the other ATM's of that bank, you might be distressed about the rather excessive delay. You might be so upset that you'll switch to another bank that can get things done much faster.

Another way to phrase things is to say that we want to ensure that the data is consistent across the distributed members. At the time that you made the $60 deposit, for a moment in time only the ATM there knows what you've done. Assuming that all the others had earlier been informed you had only $40, none of them yet know that you added $60 more. For that moment in time, we have an inconsistency. It is usually desirable to instead have consistency. You want to go to any ATM, no matter where it is, and see that your $60 deposit is known to all of those other ATM's. You want the distributed system to be consistent with respect to how much your bank account has.

If possible, you'd likely want immediate consistency, which sometimes is referred to as strong consistency. Suppose we somehow had interconnected all the bank's ATM's with super-duper fast fiber cable and within a split second of your $60 deposit it was communicated to all the others. From your perspective, it would seem as though it was instantaneous and utterly consistent. I think we can all agree though that it would still have been momentarily inconsistent, maybe just for a fraction of a second while the updates were occurring, but, meanwhile, admittedly, for practical purposes of you going to another ATM to check your balance, it sure seemed like there was no gap in time.

The principle of "eventual consistency" now can be considered in our story herein about distributed systems. Assume that we cannot achieve pure instantaneous consistency, and there's going to be some amount of delay involved of ensuring that all the distributed members are updated. I might scare you by saying that our distributed system could be designed such that it will never fully achieve consistency, meaning that some of those ATM's aren't ever going to get updated about your $100 balance. That's ugly, I realize, but it could be a possibility.

You might say to me, Lance, I can't take that, and so please promise that the distributed system has at least eventual consistency. Inevitably, even if it takes a large delay, make sure that consistency is ultimately reached. Maybe in the first few hours of your making the $60 deposit, half of the other ATM's get updated. Then, suppose after about ten hours have passed, now 90% of the ATM's are updated. By the time a 24-hour period has expired, suppose 100% of the ATM's are updated. In that sense, eventually consistency was achieved.

You might be ecstatic that the eventual consistency was ultimately achieved and the 100% update was made across the board. Meanwhile, you might be mildly concerned that during the 24-hour period, there was some stale data and the fresh data had not yet entirely propagated. For designing a distributed system, there's always a difficult trade-off of the latency (delay) time versus the staleness/freshness of the data, and the cost of the system. You ideally want the least delay to ensure the freshest data is available, but this likely comes at a high price in a non-centralized or distributed system.

Here's a typical semi-formal definition for eventual consistency: Eventual consistency is a type of distributed model approach that informally provides that for any given data item, eventually the accesses to that data item will return the latest updated value.

There is a myriad of ways to implement this notion of "eventual consistency," and also whether or not the distributed system "guarantees" that the consistency will ultimately be achieved or not. You also can characterize the distributed system as having strong consistency versus weak consistency. The designer of the distributed system needs to consider how large the distributed system is or will become, such as say having only 50 ATM's (nodes) or a massive 50,000 ATM's (nodes). How scalable does it need to be? What kind of availability is expected? How complex can it be? Etc.

What does this have to do with AI self-driving cars?

At the Cybernetic AI Self-Driving Car Institute, we are developing AI for self-driving cars, which includes designing and crafting the on-board distributed components of the self-driving car.

An AI self-driving car has tons of computer processors and tons of software components, encompassing aspects that entail the running of the car and the running of the AI, along with the numerous sensors and other devices. It's a distributed system.

Accordingly, it is important to be concerned about the "consistency" of the data that's within that distributed system.

Rather than covering further the distributed system aspects of consistency, I'd like to shift your attention toward another angle on consistency as it relates to AI self-driving cars. This will parlay into the nature of eventual consistency, per my story about banking and the ATM's.

The key aspects of the driving task for an AI self-driving car consist of:

- Sensor data collection and interpretation

- Sensor fusion

- Virtual world model updating

- AI action planning

- Car controls commands issuance

The AI self-driving car makes use of various sensors, such as cameras, radar, LIDAR, sonar, and collects data about the world surrounding the self-driving car. This data needs to be interpreted and transformed for use by the rest of the AI system. It is fed into the senor fusion portion, which tries to reconcile the multiple ways of sensing the surroundings. The camera and vision processing might spot some aspects, the radar might spot some of those same aspects and also spot other aspects that the camera did not detect, and so on. The results of the sensor fusion are fed into the virtual world model that is being kept updated, reflecting in a virtual way the surroundings.

With the virtual world model, the AI system can try to predict what will happen next. A car coming toward the self-driving car might be getting ready to turn in front of the self-driving car. If the virtual model suggests that's what is going to happen, the AI action plan component then would try to devise the action to be taken by the self-driving car. Perhaps the self-driving needs to slow down, or maybe it needs to swerve to avoid the other car. Once the AI action plan is formulated or updated, the AI system would issue car controls commands, causing the physical mechanisms of the car to turn the wheel, hit the brakes, or get the car to accelerate, as befits whatever action is intended.

While driving down a road, these driving actions are happening in a repeated cycle. The sensor data is being collected, it is fed into the sensor fusion, which is fed into the virtual world model, which is fed into the AI action planner, which feeds into the car controls commands issuance. This repeats over and over. It is taking place in real-time. And it has to happen fast enough that the self-driving car is properly and safely driving on the roadways.

The data being brought into this repeating cycle is often gradually going to reveal an overall arch of something that is taking place in a more macroscopic way.

If you look at how a teenage novice driver copes with driving, they often are only focused on the moment to moment execution of the driving task. They see what's directly ahead, they react. It's a simple monkey-see, monkey-do, kind of action. A more seasoned driver is able to deal with the moment to moment elements of driving, and also has an ability to anticipate a longer term viewpoint too. The seasoned driver might be watching traffic way up ahead, and not just looking at the bumper of the car directly in front of their car.

A novice driver tends to be confused by inconsistency. Suppose the car directly ahead of them is braking, but the car to their right is not. Shouldn't both of those cars be braking? And, if they are both braking, the novice figures maybe they should hit the brakes too. But, if only one of them is braking, maybe they shouldn't be braking. Or, maybe they should. The narrowness of the novice's viewpoint of the traffic and roadway makes it difficult to cope with what seems to be inconsistent behavior (or, if we consider the behavior as something perceived by your senses, we might then say that the data seems to be inconsistent).

Stale data becomes relevant here too. I was sitting in a car of a novice teenage driver that looked over his shoulder to see if it would be safe to make a lane change. The teenager didn't see any car in the next lane and so mentally decided it would be OK to make the lane change. Upon the teenager's gaze coming back to looking forward, he momentarily become attentive to the car ahead that was tapping its brakes. The teenager then decided that he should quickly make the lane change, avoiding possibly riding up upon the now braking car ahead. Unfortunately, in the few seconds of his looking forward, a car from a third lane had come into the lane that he wanted to get into, and now was sitting right where he would make his lane change.

The data he had in his mind was stale. It no longer reflected the reality of the situation around him. Without realizing that he needed to refresh the data, he would have for sure made the lane change and likely cut-off the other car. Worse, his car and the other car could have hit each other. I spoke up just as he started to make motions to switch lanes, and gently dissuaded him (it was a gentle caution, since I didn't want to cause a panic and have him make some dire move!).

Let's use an even larger scope example of how the consistency or inconsistency of data can emerge over time.

You are on the freeway, driving along at full speed. At first, traffic seems wide open. You then notice that there is intermittent braking taking place in the traffic up ahead. It's sporadic. Next, the braking becomes more persistent and widespread. Traffic begins to slow down. The slowing progresses to becoming slower and slower. The traffic then becomes bumper to bumper. It's now stop and go traffic. Overall, traffic is now moving at a crawl.

I'm sure you've experienced this kind of traffic before. Pretty typical, especially for a morning or evening commute.

What though do you make of this traffic situation?

If you are a novice driver, perhaps you are not thinking beyond the fact that the traffic is moving at a crawl. A more seasoned driver is likely to begin speculating about what is causing the slowing of the traffic. Is the roadway and number of lanes not sufficiently large enough for the volume of traffic? Is there a bend in the road ahead and it has caused drivers to slow down to be cautious because they cannot see what's ahead? Is there perhaps debris on the freeway and cars are slowing to avoid hitting the debris?

Suppose I told you that you could now just barely see some flashing lights up ahead. What would you now guess is happening? You'd likely be thinking that flashing lights might mean a police car, or a fire truck, or an ambulance. Any of those on the freeway and with their flashing lights on probably suggests an accident up ahead. You can't say for sure that's what is occurring, but it's a reasonable guess.

Next, I tell you that you can now see some flares and red cones on the freeway up ahead. You are now probably betting that indeed there must have been a car accident. You also are guessing that it must have happened some time ago, in that if it had just happened there wouldn't yet be cones and flares. The police or other workers that showed up must have put down the flares and cones. All of that would have taken time.

You then see that a firetruck is parked on the freeway, straddling several lanes. At this juncture, without even being able to see beyond the firetruck, you are pretty sure there's a car accident scene. It makes sense, given the clues so far.

Let's now revisit what has taken place in this example.

The initial data about the traffic was that it was flowing unimpeded. Then, the data was that the traffic was starting to use their brakes. Some cars were still going fast, some were slowing down. In a sense, you are getting data that seems "inconsistent" and you are seeking to make it become "consistent" so that you can put together a cohesive indication of what is taking place.

Part of the macroscopic overarching aspect of the AI system in an AI self-driving car is that it should be dealing with this kind of eventual consistency. There is a sprinkling of data that at first suggests an inconsistency. From this, there becomes a gradual consistency as the data is further gathered and time progresses. At any moment in time, the AI system can be in a posture of not being sure of what is going to happen next, but it can be constructing a prediction based on what has occurred so far.

The eventual consistency might gradually be achieved, such as in this scenario that led to the realization that a car accident was up ahead. Or, the eventual consistency might not be resolved. I'm sure you've had times that the traffic slowed to a crawl and you thought for sure there must be an accident up ahead, and then once you got further ahead there seemed to be no rhyme or reason why the traffic had slowed.

Some AI developers have a mindset that they assume that the AI of the self-driving car will exist in a perfect world of having all needed information and the right information, and the fresh information, whenever needed. Even a novice teenage driver knows that to not be the case. Driving involves dealing with imperfect information. Decisions must be made based on sketchy data. Patterns that might eventually arrive at a state of consistency, might not. These are important aspects that any true AI self-driving car is going to need to cope with. Eventually, for sure. Sooner, rather than later.

CHAPTER 8
MASS TRANSIT FUTURE
AND
AI SELF-DRIVING CARS

CHAPTER 8

MASS TRANSIT FUTURE
AND AI SELF-DRIVING CARS

Hop on, hop off, hop on, hop off, and repeat until you reach your destination.

Here in Southern California, a key local transit entity is called MTA (Metropolitan Transit Authority) and provides mass transit options for commuters from throughout Los Angeles county. You've got light rail, heavy rail, busses, and the like.

Of the nearly one hundred MTA stations used by commuters to get access into the transit system, it turns out that only a few of those stations directly intersect with a second line. This means that you need to hop onto one train, hop off at another station, wait for the next right train, hop on, and maybe then arrive at the final station you were intending to reach. It seems likely you'll need to make at least two or three such stops and switches, in reality, due to the lack of stations being interconnected with multiple lines.

You might say that it's no big deal and shrug it off as just part of the mass transit system here. Unfortunately, it is a big deal in that it tends to turn-off riders or potential riders. They perceive that it is too confusing to have to make so many switches. They perceive that it uses up too much time, having to make the switches and sit around for the

111

needed waiting times for the next right train. All in all, the inconvenience tips them over into avoiding using the mass transit option for travel.

The less riders on the mass transit system, the less valuable it is having the mass transit system. It also means that the lack of ridership implies there's less people taken out of the conventional car traffic pool. And, thus, the mass transit doesn't achieve some key stated goals of reducing conventional car traffic, which tends to also reduce pollution, and the mass transit is supposed to produce a lower cost alternative per mile per person traveled.

One topic being discussed and debated here in Los Angeles is the proposed development of a new north-south spine that would run throughout central L.A. and create more intersecting points with the existing stations. According to Metro, the new line would potentially serve 90,000 trips a day and become the busiest light-rail line in the United States.

If all goes well in terms of proceeding to build the new line, it would open in the year 2047.

That's right, the official ribbon cutting for the first ridership would be about 30 years from now. Yikes! For most of us, it's hard to imagine waiting thirty years for something. If you have small children, they'll be middle aged by the time the new line is running. If you are middle aged now, you'll likely be nearing retirement. If you are already retired now, I can only hope you'll be around to come and see the grand unveiling of the new line.

In terms of cost, it's estimated right now that it could be $150 million per mile (total of about $3 billion) if built at street level. Some say that it should not be at street level, and be instead placed either above ground via an aerial line, or it should go underground. These other options are more expensive, including for example that the underground approach would likely be around $700 million per mile (total project cost of $4.7 billion). These are projected costs, of which there are some critics that say it's way under-estimated and the true price tag will be much larger.

There is a group pushing to get the project done sooner and wants to have the new line underway by the time the 2028 Summer Olympics come to Los Angeles – hey, mark that year on your calendar to come visit L.A. in the year 2028. Be there, or be square.

Anyway, aiming to shave about 20 years off the 2047 forecasted date would certainly be a nice wish to have occur. But, whether you can accelerate a project of this magnitude, given all of the regulatory hurdles, the political aspects, and the rest, along with what it might due to pushing up the cost, well, let's just say it's still a dream for the moment.

Focus on the year 2047. Think seriously about it. Place your mind into the future.

What does this have to do with AI self-driving cars?

Depending upon whom you believe, we're presumably going to have quite a number of AI self-driving cars on our roadways by the time that the year 2047 rolls around. One notable prediction mentioned in a Fortune magazine article last year said that by the year 2040 that about 95% of new cars sold in the United States will be AI self-driving cars. Source: http://fortune.com/2017/09/13/gm-cruise-self-driving-driverless-autonomous-cars/

If that's the case, it would tend to suggest that by the year 2047 there will be an enormous number of AI self-driving cars cruising around our highways and byways.

Some clarifications are needed.

Right now, there are an estimated 200+ million conventional cars in the United States. Whenever AI self-driving cars start to become readily available, it will take a while to turn over the stock of conventional cars to become AI self-driving cars. I've mentioned many times that I'm doubtful there will be much in the way of kits to retrofit conventional cars, and that instead you'll need to buy a new car that's equipped as an AI self-driving car. And, since most people cannot just outright ditch their existing car and buy a new one, the odds are that it will take many years for AI self-driving cars to become widely populated on our roads.

If we go along with the notion that it won't be until about 2040 that the predominant new car purchase will consist of AI self-driving cars, it suggests that during the 2020's and the 2030's we'll have a mix of conventional cars and AI self-driving cars, but that conventional cars will still be the dominant mode of car traffic on our roads. I've emphasized this aspect many times too because there are some AI self-driving car pundits that keep bringing up a nirvana world of all and exclusively AI self-driving cars on our streets, but this just isn't going to happen for a very long time.

It's important to realize that there are various levels of AI self-driving cars. The topmost level is Level 5, which is the point at which an AI self-driving car can drive the car without any human intervention needed. Indeed, there is usually no provision in the car for any human driving, such as there is the elimination of the pedals and the steering wheel. Whatever a human could do in terms of driving the car, it is expected that the AI will do instead for a Level 5 AI self-driving car.

During the 2020's and the 2030's, we'll definitely see a lot of cars that are at the levels 2 and 3, and perhaps some at the level 4, but presumably very few at the true Level 5. There will be some intense and acrimonious debate about whether a self-driving car has actually achieved a Level 5, and which is a facet not so easily determined.

Returning to the matter at-hand, I began by mentioning that the Los Angeles mass transit authority is aiming to add a new line at a cost of perhaps $3 billion to $5 billion dollars, and that it won't be ready until 2047 (unless there's a miracle and Santa Claus that gets it done by 2028).

Here's the million dollar (or billion dollar) question: Do we need more mass transit by the time we reach the mid-2040's and beyond?

If we're going to have widespread AI self-driving cars by that same time frame, perhaps we're pouring money into added mass transit that will ultimately have been for not. In other words, yes let's keep the existing mass transit system going, since we presumably need it during the next 30 years or so for purposes of shoring up the lack of widespread AI self-driving cars, but maybe we should be doing a gut check as to starting to build something that won't come available until a future in which it maybe won't be needed.

It's perhaps a bridge to nowhere, as they say.

By the way, we already have a bridge to nowhere here in California, based in our San Gabriel mountains. Back in 1936, there was an effort to build an arch bridge that was going to connect with a road that would lead to San Gabriel Valley. The bridge got built. The road got washed out in 1938. The decision was made that it was no longer worth the cost to proceed. The bridge now just sits there. From time to time, people come to look at it and some try to parachute off it. It's officially known as the "Bridge to Nowhere."

In any case, any mass transit project that is going to get started now or in the near future, and for which it might take 30 years or more to get built, we probably should look in the mirror and say do we like what we see? Does it make sense to pump money into such projects?

One argument in favor of proceeding on the mass transit project would be that we don't really know when the advent will be of AI self-driving cars in terms of a timeline, and thus it's a reasonable hedge bet to assume that mass transit will still be needed by 2047. It's conceivable that we won't have many AI self-driving cars by then, and instead maybe it will be another twenty or thirty years later, such as perhaps 2060 or 2070. In that case, plow ahead with more mass transit until we reach those later dates.

Another argument in favor of proceeding would be that even if AI self-driving cars are popular by 2047, maybe we will still need mass transit.

Let's consider that aspect, pro and con.

Some believe that with the prevalence of AI self-driving cars, we are going to have a ridesharing-as-an-economy way of living. This means that ridesharing will be the dominant mode of travel and that we'll be using AI self-driving cars to do so. Those that buy AI self-driving cars will realize that they don't need to use it 24x7, even though it can be used 24x7 generally because it has an electronic chauffer always at the ready. So, people will turn their AI self-driving car into a ridesharing service. Some will purchase an AI self-driving car purposely to be a ridesharing service and use it almost entirely and only for making money as a ridesharing mechanism.

If that happens, would anyone want to use mass transit? Instead they can use a car that provides their own bubble, it will take them directly where they want to go, they don't need to wait to use it, and presumably the cost will be relatively low since there will such a huge supply of these AI self-driving cars.

Furthermore, the AI self-driving car can cover the last mile for them – this is a reference to the problem that most mass transit options can't get you to your actual desired destination. You need to get from a train station to that grocery store or your home, and so the mass transit isn't complete. Meanwhile, the AI self-driving car could take you on the short hauls and even the longer hauls, in theory.

You might argue that all those AI self-driving cars will be polluting and gas guzzlers, which is the reason why mass transit is better, ecologically. But, the odds are that most if not all AI self-driving cars are going to be electrical vehicles. Therefore, no gas guzzling, and little or no pollutants. The mass transit ecological argument is valid today because we have so many conventional cars and they are pretty much gas fueled. It seems unlikely that's the way that AI self-driving cars will be.

The aforementioned aspects seem to suggest that we won't need mass transit. That might seem harsh. Suppose instead we say that we'll need less mass transit, but not eliminate it entirely. There will still be circumstances perhaps of not wanting to use an AI self-driving car and instead ride on a train or a bus.

We also need to consider that presumably if the AI is good enough to drive a car, it would seem to be good enough to likely drive a bus, and drive a train. In that case, we've taken the labor costs out of the bus driving and the train driving. This perhaps makes mass transit even more affordable.

In the United States, there is about $65 billion spent annually toward the mass transit systems. The average trip length is around 5.5 miles. There are an estimated 433,000 people employed by mass transit in America, of which 97% of them are in the operational aspects of mass transit. These are numbers provided by the American Public Transportation Association (APTA).

If AI self-driving cars cause mass transit to disappear or dramatically scale-down, presumably this would mean that the $65 billion being spent today would possibly go to other uses. What would happen to the nearly half a million people employed by mass transit? Seemingly, hopefully, the ramp down of mass transit would occur over a lengthy enough period that those people would be able to shift to some other area of the economy.

According to the mass transit industry, for each $1 billion added investment in mass transit, those invested dollars supports the creation of potentially 50,000 jobs. If we once again assume the scenario of not making those mass transit investments, at least for investments involving mass transit that won't come on-line until 2047 or thereabouts, it suggests that those added jobs can't be counted on to materialize.

Might the advent of AI self-driving cars generate the same kind of jobs expansion, in lieu of the mass transit?

Maybe. With all of those AI self-driving cars, and going around the clock, there's going to be a lot of need for maintenance and upkeep of those cars. A car is still a car. It will breakdown. Probably even more so than now, since the self-driving cars might be run all the time. Presumably, lots of human specialists for doing maintenance and repairs will be needed, at least until it can be automated via robotics or similar.

Today, there are an estimated 5% of cars in the United States that are being used for ridesharing. By the year 2040, some predictions are that 68% of cars will be used for ridesharing. This opens up a tremendous capacity for doing ridesharing. It seems like it has to take away ridership from someplace else, and thus mass transit seems like one place that gets reduced in terms of ridership as it shifts over to the AI self-driving cars.

There are some that insist we'll see induced demand working in this future situation regarding travel. People today that don't travel, or only travel to some degree N, they will all now opt to travel and do so for some heightened amount Z. If you believe in that notion, it could be that with such a massive scaling up of demand for travel, the mass transit still remains in place. We might need both the advent of AI self-driving cars and the ongoing capability of mass transit to handle all of that gargantuan demand.

Over the last 20 years or so, the growth of mass transit passenger miles has eclipsed the number of car miles traveled. Mass transit though still only is used by a relatively small percentage of the traveling public. With the emergence and ultimately prevalence of AI self-driving cars, it might seem reasonable to anticipate that the number of car miles traveled will not only eclipse the mass transit passenger miles, but do so by perhaps a dramatic amount.

We also need to consider the opportunity costs associated with spending on future mass transit expansions. If the Los Angeles line expansion gets the needed $3 to $5 billion dollars in spending, of which some will come from local sources and some from federal (maybe half from federal), could that money have been put to some other use instead? If it's a bridge to nowhere, maybe there's other projects that would be a wiser investment. On the other hand, since the billions will be spent over the next thirty years, you could at least say that it has had a benefit of hiring the people that did the construction during that period of time (and other side economic benefits).

These speculations involve all sorts of economic guesses and also technological guesses.

When will AI self-driving cars become prevalent? Will they be as safe as mass transit? Will they be as reliable? Will they be more or less costly than mass transit?

I'm sure you've heard the phrase "voodoo economics" having been used, often in a condescending way, when referring to speculative economic theories that are being espoused. For AI self-driving cars, perhaps we've got a bit of "voodoo predictions" about when AI self-driving cars will truly be viable and become a mainstay in society. Whether or not we should bet on the future of mass transit based on the voodoo predictions is a tough call. Some say play it safe and build a potential bridge to nowhere, in case it turns out to be a bridge to somewhere, while others decry this kind of logic and say don't put good money after bad. Guess we need time to let this play out, and maybe a witch doctor to sort this out.

.

CHAPTER 9
COOPETITION AND
AI SELF-DRIVING CARS

CHAPTER 9

COOPETITION AND
AI SELF-DRIVING CARS

Competitors usually fight tooth and nail for every inch of ground they can gain over the other. It's a dog eat dog world and if you can gain an advantage over your competition, so the better you shall be. If you can even somehow drive your competition out of business, well, as long as it happened legally, there's more of the pie for you.

Given this rather obvious and strident desire to beat your competition, it might seem like heresy to suggest that you might at times consider backing down from being at each other's throats and instead, dare I say, possibly cooperate with your competition. You might not be aware that the US Postal Service (USPS) has cooperative arrangements with FedEx and UPS – on the surface this seems wild to think that these competitors, obviously all directly competing as shippers, would consider working together rather than solely battling each other.

Here's another example, Wintel. For those of you in the tech arena, you know well that Microsoft and Intel have seemingly forever cooperated with each other. The Windows and Intel mash-up, Wintel, has been pretty good for each of them respectively and collectively. When Intel's chips became more powerful, it aided Microsoft in speeding up Windows and being able to add more features and heavier ones. As people used Windows and wanted faster speed and greater capabilities, it sparked Intel to boost their chips, knowing there was a place to sell them, and make more money by doing so.

You could say it is a synergistic relationship between those two firms that in combination has aided them both.

Now, I realize you might object somewhat and insist that Microsoft and Intel are not competitors per se, thus, the suggestion that this was two competitors that found a means to cooperate seems either an unfair characterization or a false one. You'd be somewhat on the mark to have noticed that they don't seem to be direct competitors, though they could be if they wanted to do so (Microsoft could easily get into the chip business, Intel could easily get into the OS business, and they've both dabbled in each other's pond from time-to-time). Certainly, though it's not as strong straight-ahead competition example as would be the USPS, FedEx, UPS kind of cooperative arrangement.

There's a word used to depict the mash-up of competition and cooperation, namely coopetition.

You don't hear the word coopetition used much. It grew into some prominence in the 1990s, but otherwise seems to rarely get much attention. Some people instantly react to the notion of being both a competitor and a cooperator as though it's a crazy idea. What, give away my secrets to my competition, are you nuts? Indeed, trying to pull-off a coopetition can be tricky, as I'll describe further herein.

Some instantly recoil in horror at the idea of coopetition and their knee jerk reaction is that it must be utterly illegal. They assume that there must be laws that prevent such a thing. Generally, depending upon how the coopetition is arranged, there's nothing illegal about it per se. The coopetition can though veer in a direction that raises legal concerns and thus the participants need to be especially careful about what they do, how they do it, and what impact it has on the marketplace.

It's not particularly the potential for legal difficulties that tends to keep coopetition from happening. By and large, the means to structure a coopetition arrangement, via say putting together a consortium, it can be done with relatively little effort and cost. The real question and the bigger difficulty is whether the competing firms are able to find middle ground that allows them to enter into a coopetition agreement.

Think about today's major high-tech firms.

Most of them are run by strong CEO's or founders that relish being bold and love smashing their competition. They often drive their firm to have a kind of intense "hatred" for the competition and want their firm to crush the competition. Within a firm, there is often a cultural milieu formed that their firm is far superior, and the competition is unquestionably inferior. Your firm is a winner, the competing firm is a loser. That being said, they don't want you to let down your guard, in the sense that though the other firm is an alleged loser, they can pop-up at any moment and be on the attack, so you need to be on your guard. To some degree, there's a begrudging respect for the competition, paradoxically mixed with disdain for the competition.

These strong personalities will generally tend to keep the competitive juices going and not permit the possibility of a coopetition option. On the other hand, even these strong personalities can be motivated to consider the coopetition approach, if the circumstances or the deal looks attractive enough. With a desire to get bigger and stronger, if it seems like a coopetition could get you there, the most egocentric of leaders is willing to give the matter some thought. Of course, it's got to be incredibly compelling, but at least it is worthy of consideration and not out of hand to float the idea.

What could be compelling?

Here's a number for you, $7 trillion dollars.

Allow me to explain.

At the Cybernetic AI Self-Driving Car Institute, we are developing AI software for self-driving cars. We do so because it's going to be a gargantuan market, and because it's exciting to be creating something that's on par with a moonshot.

Suppose you were the head of a car maker, or the head of a high-tech firm that wanted or is making tech for cars, and I told you that the potential market for AI self-driving cars is estimated at $7 trillion dollars by the year 2050 (as predicted in Fortune magazine, see: http://fortune.com/2017/06/03/autonomous-vehicles-market/).

That's right, I said $7 trillion dollars. It's a lot of money. It's a boatload, and more, of money. The odds are that you would want to do whatever you could to get a piece of that action. Even a small slice, let's say just a few percentages, would make your firm huge.

Furthermore, consider things from the other side of that coin. Suppose you don't get a piece of that pie. Whatever else you are doing is likely to become crumbs. If you are making conventional cars, the odds are that few will want to buy them anymore. There are some AI self-driving car pundits that are even suggesting that conventional cars would be outlawed by 2050.

The logic is that if you have conventional cars being driven by humans on our roadways in the 2050's, it will muck up the potential nirvana of having all AI self-driving cars that presumably will be able to work in unison and thus get us to the vaunted zero fatalities goal.

If you are a high-tech firm and you've not gotten into the AI self-driving car realm, your fear is that you'll also miss out on the $7 trillion dollar prize. Suppose that your high-tech competitor got into AI self-driving cars early on and they became the standard, kind of like how there was a fight between VHS and Betamax. Maybe it's wisest to get into things early and become the standard.

Or, alternatively, maybe the early arrivers will waste a lot of money trying to figure out what to do, so instead of falling into that trap, you wait on the periphery, avoiding the drain of resources, and then jump in once the others have flailed around. Many in Silicon Valley seem to believe that you have to be the first into a new realm. This is actually a false awareness since many of the most prominent firms in many areas weren't there first, they instead came along somewhat after others had poked and tried and based on the heels of those true first attempts did the other firm step in and become a household name.

Let's return to the notion of coopetition. I assume we can agree that generally the auto makers aren't very likely to want to be cooperative with each other and usually consider themselves head-on competitors.

I realize there have been exceptions, such as the deal that PSA Peugeot Citroen and Toyota made to produce the Peugeot 107 and the Toyota Aygo, but those such arrangements are somewhat sparse. Likewise, the high-tech firms tend to strive towards being competitive with each other, rather than cooperative. Again, there are exceptions such as a willingness to serve on groups that are putting together standards and protocols for various architectural and interface aspects (think of the World Wide Web Consortium, W3C, as an example).

We've certainly already seen that auto makers and high-tech firms are willing to team-up for the AI self-driving cars realm.

In that sense, it's kind of akin to the Wintel type of arrangement. I don't think we'd infer they are true coopetition arrangements since they weren't especially competing to begin with. Google's Waymo has teamed up with Chrysler to outfit the Pacifica minivans with AI self-driving car aspects. Those two firms weren't especially competitors. I realize you could assert that Google could get into the car business and be an auto maker if it wanted to, which is quite the case and they could buy their way in or even start something from scratch. You could also assert that Chrysler is doing it's own work on high-tech aspects for AI self-driving cars and in that manner might be competing with Waymo. It just doesn't though quite add-up to them being true competitors per se, at least not right now.

So, let's put to the side the myriad of auto maker and high-tech firm cooperatives underway and say that we aren't going to label those as coopetitions. Again, I realize you can argue the point and might say that even if they aren't competitors today, they could become competitors a decade from now. Yes, I get that. Just go along with me on this for now and we can keep in mind the future possibilities too.

Consider these thought provoking questions:

- Could we get the auto makers to come together into a coopetition arrangement to establish the basis for AI self-driving cars?

- Could we get the high-tech firms to come together into a coopetition arrangement to establish the basis for AI self-driving cars?

- Could we get the auto makers and tech firms that are already in bed with each other to altogether come together to enter into a coopetition arrangement?

I get asked these questions during a number of my industry talks. There are some that believe the goal of achieving AI self-driving cars is so crucial for society, so important for the benefit of mankind, that it would be best if all of these firms could come together, shake hands, and forge the basis for AI self-driving cars.

Why would these firms be willing to do this? Shouldn't they instead be wanting to "win" and become the standard for AI self-driving cars? The tempting $7 trillion dollars is a pretty alluring pot of gold. Seems premature to already throw in the towel and allow other firms to grab a piece of the pie. Maybe your efforts will knock them out of the picture. You'll have the whole kit and caboodle yourself.

Those proposing a coopetition notion for AI self-driving cars are worried that the rather "isolated" attempts by each of the auto makers and the tech firms is going either lead to failure in terms of true AI self-driving cars, or it will stretch out for a much longer time than needed.

Suppose you could have true AI self-driving cars by the year 2030, if you did a coopetition deal, versus that suppose it wasn't until 2050 or 2060 that true AI self-driving cars would emerge. This means that for perhaps 20 or 30 years there could have been true AI self-driving cars, doing so to the benefit of us all, and yet we let it slip off due to being "selfish" and allowing the AI self-driving car makers to duke it out.

You've likely see science fictions movies about a giant meteor that is going to strike earth and destroy all that we have, or an alien force from Mars that is heading to earth and likely to enslave us all. In those cases, there has been a larger foe to contend with. As such, it got all of the countries of the world to set aside their differences and band together to try and defeat the larger foe. I'm not saying that would happen in real life, and perhaps instead everyone would tear each other apart, but anyway, let's go with the happy face scenario and say that when faced with tough times, we could get together those that otherwise despise each other or see each other as their enemies, and they would become cooperative.

That's what some want to have happen in the AI self-driving cars realm. The bigger foe is the number of annual fatalities due to car accidents. The bigger foe also includes the issue of a lack of democratization of mobility, which is what it is hoped that AI self-driving cars will bring forth, a greater democratization. The bigger foe is the need to increase mobility for those that aren't able to be mobile. In other words, the basket of benefits for AI self-driving cars, and the basket of woes that it will overturn, the belief is that for those reasons the auto makers and tech firms should band together into a coopetition.

Game theory comes to play in coopetition.

If you believe in a zero-sum game, whereby the pie is just one size and those that get a bigger piece of the pie are doing so at the loss of others that will get a smaller piece of the pie, the win-lose perspective makes it hard to consider participating in a coopetition. On the other hand, if it could be a win-win possibility, whereby the pie can be made bigger, and thus the participants each get sizable pieces of pie, it makes being in the coopetition seemingly more sensible.

How would things fare in the AI self-driving cars realm? Suppose that an auto maker X that has teamed up with high-tech firm Y, they are the XY team, and they are frantically trying to be the first with a true AI self-driving car. Meanwhile, we've got auto maker Q and its high-tech partner firm Z, and so the QZ team is also frantically trying to put together a true AI self-driving car.

Would XY be willing to get into a coopetition with QZ, and would QZ want to get into a coopetition with XY?

If XY believes they need no help and will be able to achieve an AI self-driving car and do so on a timely basis and possibly beat the competition, it seems unlikely they would perceive value in doing the coopetition. You can say the same about QZ, namely, if they think they are going to be the winner, there's little incentive to get into the coopetition.

Some would argue that they could potentially shave on costs of trying to achieve an AI self-driving car by joining together. Pool resources. Do R&D together. They could possibly do some kind of technology transfer amongst each other, with one having gotten more advanced in some area than the other, and thus they trade with each on the things they each have gotten farthest along on. There's a steep learning curve on the latest in AI and so the XY and QZ could perhaps boost each other up that learning curve. Seems like the benefits of being in a coopetition are convincing.

And, it is already the case that these auto makers and tech firms are eyeing each other. They each are intently desirous of knowing how far along the other is. They are hiring away key people from each other. Some would even say there is industrial espionage underway. Plus, in some cases, there are AI self-driving car developers that appear to have stepped over the line and stolen secrets about AI self-driving cars.

This coopetition is not so easy to arrange, let alone to even consider. You are the CEO of the auto maker X, which has already forged a relationship with the high-tech firm Y. The marketplace perceives that you are doing the right thing and moving forward with AI self-driving cars. This is a crucial perception for any auto maker, since we've already seen that the auto makers will get drummed by the marketplace, such as their shares dropping, if they don't seem to be committed to achieving an AI self-driving car. It's become a key determiner for the auto maker and its leadership.

The marketplace figures that your firm, you the auto maker, will be able to achieve AI self-driving cars and that consumers will flock to your cars. Consumers will be delighted that you have AI self-driving cars. The other auto makers will fall far behind in terms of sales as everyone switches over to you. In light of that expectation, it would be somewhat risky to come out and say that you've decided to do a coopetition with your major competitors.

I'd bet that there would be a stock drop as the marketplace reacted to this approach. If all the auto makers were in the coopetition, I suppose you could say that the money couldn't flow anywhere else anyway.

On the other hand, if only some of the auto makers were in the coopetition, it would force the marketplace into making a bet. You might put your money into the auto makers that are in the coopetition, under the belief they will succeed first, or you might put your money into the other auto makers that are outside the coopetition, under the belief they will win and win bigger because they aren't having to share the pie.

Speaking of which, what would be the arrangement for the coopetition? Would all of the members participating have equal use of the AI self-driving car technologies developed? Would they be in the coopetition forever or only until a true AI self-driving car was achieved, or until some other time or ending state? Could they take whatever they got from the coopetition and use it in whatever they wanted, or would there be restrictions? And so on.

I'd bet that the coopetition would have a lot of tension. There is always bound to be professional differences of opinion. A member of the coopetition might believe that LIDAR is essential to achieving a true AI self-driving car, while some other member says they don't believe in LIDAR and see it as a false hope and a waste of time. How would the coopetition deal with this?

Normally, a coopetition is likely to be formulated when the competitors are willing to find a common means to contend with something that is relatively non-strategic to their core business. If you believe that AI self-driving cars are the future of the automobile, it's hard to see that it wouldn't be considered strategic to the core business. Indeed, even though today we don't necessarily think of AI self-driving cars as a strategic core per se, because it's still so early in the life cycle, anyone with a bit of vision can see that soon enough it will be.

If the auto makers did get together in a coopetition, and they all ended-up with the same AI self-driving car technology, how else would they differentiate themselves in the marketplace?

I realize you can say that even today the auto makers are pretty much the same in the sense that they offer a car that has an engine and has a transmission, etc. The "technology" you might say is about the same, and yet they do seem to differentiate each other. Often, the differentiation is more on style of the car, the looks of the car, rather than the tech side of things.

For those that believe that the AI part of the self-driving car will end-up being the same for cars of the future, and it won't be a differentiator to the marketplace, this admittedly makes the case for banding into a coopetition on the high-tech stuff. If the auto makers believe that the AI will be a commodity item, why not get into a coopetition, figure this arcane high-tech AI stuff out, and be done with it. No sense in fighting over something that anyway is going to be generic across the board.

At this time, it appears that the auto makers believe they can reach a higher value by creating their own AI self-driving car, doing so in conjunction with a particular high-tech firm that they've chosen, rather than doing so via a coopetition.

Some have wondered if we'll see a high-tech firm that opts to build its own car, maybe from scratch, but so far that doesn't seem to be the case (in spite of the rumors about Apple, for example). There are some firms that are developing both the car and the high-tech themselves, such as Tesla, and see no need to band with another firm, as yet.

Right now, the forces appear to be swayed toward the don't side of doing a coopetition. Things could change. Suppose that no one is able to achieve a true AI self-driving car? It could be that the pressures become large enough (the bigger foe) that they auto makers and tech firms consider the coopetition notion.

Or, maybe the government decides to step in and forces some kind of coopetition, doing so under the belief that it is a societal matter and regulatory guidance is needed to get us to true AI self-driving cars. Or, maybe indeed aliens from Mars start to head here and we realize that if we just had AI self-driving cars we'd be able to fend them off.

There's the old line about if you can't beat them, join them. For the moment, it's assumed that the ability to beat them is greater than the join them alternative. The year 2050 is still off in the future and anything might happen on the path to that $7 trillion dollars.

CHAPTER 10
ELECTRIC VEHICLES
AND
AI SELF-DRIVING CARS

CHAPTER 10

ELECTRIC VEHICLES
AND
AI SELF-DRIVING CARS

Electrical Vehicles (EVs) are talked about, they are praised, they get a lot of attention, and in some parts of the United States there is a near obsession with them (hint: California). In spite of all the hype and press, the reality is that there are only around 1 million such cars in the U.S. and it represents a small fraction therefore of the 200+ million cars in the country. That's less than one-half of one percent of the total cars in circulation.

When I say this at various industry presentations, those with an EV are quick to yell at me as a traitor and get upset at my seemingly naysayer commentary. Allow me to clarify that I am fully supportive of EVs and hope that a lot more will get sold. I'm a big cheerleader for EVs. All I'm trying to point out is that we have a long way to go before they become prevalent.

Indeed, let me say this, please go out and buy an EV tomorrow!

Okay, no more of the traitorous talk, if you will. In terms of EVs, I am lumping together all variations in this herein discussion, for convenience sake. Generally, there are Plug-in EV's (PEVs), consisting of Battery EV (BEVs) that are equipped to only run on batteries, and there are the Hybrid EVs (abbreviated as either HEVs or PHEVs), which use both a gas powered internal combustion engine and battery power.

Why have EV's?

One argument in favor of EV is that they are less polluting than conventional gas-powered cars. Thus, ecologically, the EV is better for the environment. We can all breath a bit easier.

Another argument is that the adoption of EV's might aid in reducing the pace of climate change. That's one that gets a lot of people in a tizzy since there are some that believe in climate change and some that do not. Anyway, I'm listing it for completeness and you can decide if you think it's a bona fide element or not.

EV's would reduce the dependence on oil and the production of gasoline. This would seem like a handy move since there are various predictions about how costly it is coming to become to get oil and make gasoline. Presumably it's a limited resource and we're using it up. Also, it obviously tends to provide power to those that have it and not so much to those that don't. Some say down with the cartels.

Another less discussed aspect in favor of EVs is that people like the quietness and the feel of driving an EV. I'm going to list that as an argument in favor of EVs, but I realize not everyone necessarily likes that aspect. There are some that love the sound of a conventional combustion engine and refuse to get an EV because it doesn't have the same sound and fury. To each their own.

The government right now is offering incentives to have people buy EVs, so from that perspective the government is somewhat supportive of EVs, which helps to promote them and keep the price lower than what it might otherwise be.

This takes us to the negatives about EVs.

Some would say they are too expensive. Plus, if the government reduces the incentives to get one, it will be even more costly. Of course, the counter-argument is that we are still in the early days of EVs and eventually the cost will come down.

The auto makers are right now generally taking it on the chin to develop, make, and sell EVs. For example, the news reports that the Chevrolet Bolt is allegedly being sold at a loss. The Nissan Leaf has been rumored to not being making a profit. I think it's fair to say that right now all the auto makers that are into EVs are finding themselves faced with razor sharp margins and it's quite a feat to find a profit in this.

That being said, one could look at this as a wide-open market. It's poised to explode. Currently in its infancy, one would expect that the adoption rate is low and the costs are high at the start of any new innovation adoption. At some point, the popularity goes up and the price will be coming down. Most would claim that they can see on the horizon a mass market electric car that turns a nice profit.

Sometimes you've got to invest in something at a loss, being patient before it turns around and hopefully becomes a true money maker. The auto makers have to play the game since otherwise, if the market does become EV crazed, each auto maker will need to have its own EV for consumers to buy. Imagine if the EV market booms and you are the only auto maker that didn't have the foresight and fortitude to put together an EV. That would be bad news for you, for your company, for your shareholders, etc.

You could add that having an EV is considered politically correct too. For some people, they enjoy bragging about their EV. It is considered stylish. Want a piece of the future, today? Get yourself an EV.

There are political analysts that worry about which country will get into EV first. China right now is going gangbusters over EV. China's BYD and BAIC lead the pack in EV sales over the last year. Should we look at dollars or should we look at units sold? There are some focusing on luxury EVs, notably having a much higher price tag than the everyday EV. There are arguments about which auto maker is in the lead, depending upon your metric of using dollar sales volume versus number of units sold.

What does this have to do with AI self-driving cars?

At the Cybernetic AI Self-Driving Car Institute, we are developing AI software for self-driving cars. Doing so also makes us aware of the electrical power needs of an AI self-driving car.

During my presentations at industry conferences, attendees often assume that all AI self-driving cars will be EVs. There is a bit of shock when I point out that this is not necessarily the case.

Here's what people seem to say:

- EVs will be the cause of AI self-driving cars, without which there won't be AI self-driving cars.

- AI self-driving cars will be the cause of EVs, without which there won't be EVs.

Neither of those statements make much sense when you take them apart or unpack them.

Let's tackle the notion that EVs will be the cause of AI self-driving cars (and, the added corollary that without EVs there won't be AI self-driving cars). It's kind of a hyper claim that mishmashes things together.

We'll begin with some fundamentals. An AI self-driving car has lots of sensory devices, such as cameras, radar, sonic, LIDAR, and the rest. These all require electrical power to run. An AI self-driving car has lots of computer processors and memory devices which are needed to run the AI part of things. These all require electric power to run. It's readily apparent that an AI self-driving car needs a lot of electrical power in order to work. Not much debate on that.

Where is the AI part of the self-driving car going to get all of this needed electrical power? Somehow, the car has to generate it.

If you use a conventional gas-powered car, you'll need to outfit the car with additional electrical generation and power storage capabilities to meet the demand of the AI and its sensors. This can be done. You can argue that it raises the cost of the gas-powered car, which that's true, and you can argue that it will take up space in the car, which is also true. So, yes, a conventional gas-powered car might need to chew-up the trunk space to have added batteries and electrical elements, and overall the cost of the car is likely to go up. All true.

The point is that it doesn't preclude the use of a gas-powered car to be used for an AI self-driving car platform. It just means that a gas-powered car is perhaps a less amenable choice.

There are some that trying desperately to create kits that could turn a conventional gas-powered car into an AI self-driving car, which if this could be done would be a bonanza since you could sell the kit to presumably the 200+ million car owners in the US today. Unfortunately, the kits are not likely to be viable, mainly because of the add-on needed to a conventional car, and not solely having to do with the electrical power constraints.

So, let's go ahead an reject the notion that AI self-driving cars are not possible without EVs. That just doesn't ring true.

The first part of the statement was that EVs will cause the advent of AI self-driving cars. That's only half true, I'd say.

I think its fair to say that even if EVs didn't exist that we would all still be pouring our hearts into trying to create AI self-driving cars. The electrical power aspect is for most AI developers an afterthought. They aren't worried about whether this machine learning system or that AI code is going to require a heftier processor that consumes more power. Their assumption is that the power will be found. It's up to those clever automotive engineers to get them the power needed.

I remember when smart phones first came out. The amount of available battery power was negligible. It seemed as though if you used your smart phone for the running of a game app for a few minutes and if you made a phone call or text, voila you were out of power. Power consumption really wasn't much concern per se. Of course, consumers were irked and the makers of the smart phones woke-up and realized that consumers would choose possibly one brand over another based on how long the battery lasted. This launched an intense interest in the battery makers and also how to optimize the OS for the lengthening of the battery life.

I'd wager the same is going to happen with AI self-driving cars. At first, they'll chew-up electrical power like they need the Hoover Dam or a nuclear reactor. Once it's been shown they the AI is working and we believe in self-driving cars, the attention will shift toward using less power when possible and extending the batteries of the self-driving car as long as possible. That's though a second or third step in the evolution of things.

Thus, I don't think you can say that the rise of EVs will "cause" the advent of AI self-driving cars. The word "cause" is a pretty strong one. If I stand next to you, and I shove you, and you fall to the ground, I'll grant you that I "caused" you to fall down. On the other hand, if I stand next to you, and you happen to fall down, and my standing next to you was a contributor (maybe you thought I was going to shove you and so you preempted it by dropping to the ground), I'd say that I was involved and there was some kind of correlation or relationship between the two aspects, but one wasn't the cause for the other per se.

The advent of EVs is going to make the production of an AI self-driving car easier and hopefully less costly. This is due to the aspect that the EV is already geared up to produce and store quantities of electrical power. Therefore, the AI systems and sensors can tap into it. Or, if it is needed to boost the electrical capabilities for aiding the added AI components, it would seem a natural extension of what the EV already has for its design and construction.

You can also perhaps say that without the advent of EVs, it would likely make the advent of AI self-driving cars harder, more costly, and maybe even delay their rise. Trying to graft onto a conventional gas-powered car the needed electrical storage and generation might distract from the AI side of things. The power engineers might say to the AI developers that they need to cut back on things. A conventional car might need to be redesigned and maybe even made to be bulkier or more awkward in shape and weight. Those are bad and unfortunate possibilities, but none of those would kill the desire to get to an AI self-driving car.

I'd dare say that there is such an intense desire to get to an AI self-driving car that if needed the auto makers would start over and make some kind of new car to accommodate it. This doesn't seem to be needed as yet. So far, it appears that with pretty much a normal car, whether an EV or a gas-powered one, we'll be able to make it into an AI self-driving car.

And, though the EV advocates will get angry at me, I'd claim there is as much if not even more calls for an AI self-driving car than there is for an EV. Ouch, I said it.

People kind of buy into the EV advantages of the environment and all the rest, but it doesn't seem to pique their interest. It's a car that happens to use electricity. Nice. That's a good thing. On the other hand, if you tell someone that we can make a self-driving car, which will drive you whenever you want, and you don't need to drive the car, it's something that people say, yeh, I want one of those. It has the draw of allowing for a sense of freedom. It will provide mobility for the masses. It will change the nature of society. An EV is not going to do the same, sorry.

This brings us to the other statement that I had mentioned earlier, namely the claim that perhaps AI self-driving cars will bring about the advent of EVs, or as stated "cause" it to occur.

Kind of.

As I've already mentioned, it is not a precondition that an AI self-driving car can only happen if the car itself is an EV. There isn't a requirement that the underlying car must be an EV. If it was the case that only an EV would suffice, I'd say that there would be even more strenuous efforts to get the world toward EV, as being sparked by the desire to get us to an AI self-driving car.

Will AI self-driving cars spur the advent of EV? Yes, I think we can say that without much reservation or qualification. The alignment of the need of the AI to have lots of electrical power with an underlying platform made for that purpose, the two will certainly fit like a glove.

They will go hand-in-hand, as it were.

I'll once again quibble with the notion that the AI self-driving car will cause EV adoption. If the AI self-driving car makers opt to use EV as the underlying platform, and if the sales of those self-driving cars goes through the roof, due to the AI part of things, I'm not sure if we'd call that a cause-and-effect per se. Anyway, with the rising tide, all boats rise, as they say.

We probably should also consider the other side of the coins on this discussion about EVs and AI self-driving cars.

Suppose that we aren't able to achieve a true AI self-driving car? Meanwhile, suppose that the auto makers and tech firms have been using EVs as the primary platform for this AI self-driving car attempts. Could this hurt the advent of EVs? Maybe people would get confused and inextricably consider the AI and the EV as one thing. Thus, if the AI doesn't cut the mustard, perhaps consumers would partially blame the EV side. Out goes the baby with the bath water.

Suppose the EVs cannot come down in cost and remain relatively expensive. If the AI self-driving car is tagged on top of the EV, it presumably now becomes even more expensive. Would this price out the AI self-driving car for the masses? Would people perceive the AI self-driving car as an elitist toy? This could generate a backlash against AI self-driving cars.

Another consideration is the range of the EV. If it is consuming electrical power to run the car and to run the AI portions, it might need to frequently stop at a charging station to recharge. If you add to this the notion that many believe most AI self-driving cars will be used non-stop 24x7, and that they will become a dominant ridesharing mechanism, the cost to stop and thus loss money while sitting there and charging, well, it is going to hurt. In spite of the downsides about gasoline, the length of time to fill-up is minimal and the distance drivable is high.

The EV world is working on these aspects of reducing the charging time and maximizing the distance an EV can go. Meanwhile, though, its another consideration about having an AI self-driving car that becomes intertwined with an EV platform.

Since the EV and the AI self-driving car might be perceived as joined at the hip, given that both are rising up at about the same time, whatever happens to one can spill over into the other. Imagine an AI self-driving car that goes awry and kills someone. Will consumers and the public realize that this is perhaps due to the AI and has nothing to do with the EV? If the public cannot separate the two, it could cause a blackeye on EV, even though this would presumably be completely unfair and unwarranted.

Sometimes when I'm on a plane flying to give a speech, the person in the seat next to me will be curious when I say that I'm in the midst of developing AI self-driving cars. They often will say something like they wish they too had an electric car, stating as such under the assumption that EV and AI self-driving cars are one and the same. The odds are that they will be, and we can pretty much go along with the idea that AI self-driving cars are going to be EVs. I usually just smile and mumble that yes, EVs are cool. For those of you doing the automotive power engineering, as an AI developer, all I can say is "Scotty, we need more power" (in the immortal words of Captain Kirk). I thank you in-advance for doing so.

CHAPTER 11

DANGERS OF IN-MOTION
AI SELF-DRIVING CARS

CHAPTER 11

DANGERS OF IN-MOTION AI SELF-DRIVING CARS

I'm hoping that you have not tried to do the so-called Shiggy Challenge. If you haven't done it, I further hope that my telling you about it does not somehow spark you to go ahead and try doing it. For those of you that don't know about it and have not a clue about what it is, be ready to be "amazed" at what is emerging as a social media generated fad. It's a dangerous one.

Here's the deal.

You are supposed to get out of a moving car, leaving the driver's seat vacant, and do a dance while nearby to the continually moving forward car, and video record your dancing (you are also moving forward at the same pace as the moving car), and then jump back into the car to continue driving it.

If you ponder this for a moment, I trust that you instantly recognize the danger of this and (if I might say) the stupidity of it (or does that make me appear to be old-fashioned?).

As you might guess, already there have been people that hurt themselves while trying to jump out of the moving car, spraining an ankle, hurting a knee, banging their legs on the door, etc. Likewise, they have gotten hurt while trying to jump back into the moving car (collided with the steering wheel or the seat arm, etc.).

There are some people that while dancing outside the moving car became preoccupied and didn't notice that their moving car was heading toward someone or something. Or, they weren't themselves moving forward fast enough to keep pace with the moving car. And so on. There have been reported cases of the moving car blindly hitting others and also in some cases hitting a parked car or other objects near or in the roadway.

Some of the videos show the person having gotten out of their car and then the car door closing unexpectedly, and, guess what, the car turns out to now have all the car doors locked. Thus, the person could not readily get back into the car to stop it from going forward and potentially hitting someone or something.

This is one of those seemingly bizarre social media fads that began somewhat innocently and then the ante got upped with each person seeking fame by adding more danger to it. As you know, people will do anything to try and get views. The bolder your video, the great the chance it will go viral.

This challenge began in a somewhat simple way. The song "In My Feelings" by Drake was released and at about the same time there was a video made by an on-line personality named Shiggy that showed Shiggy taking a video of himself dancing to the tune (posted on his Instagram site). Other personalities and celebrities then opted to do the same dance, video recording themselves dancing to the Drake song, and they posted their versions. This spawned a mild viral sensation of doing this.

But, as with most things on social media, there became a desire to do something more outlandish. At first, this involved being a passenger in a slowly moving car, getting out, doing the Shiggy inspired dance, and then jumping back in. This is obviously not recommended, though at least there was still a human driver at the wheel. This then morphed into the driver being the one to jump out, and either having a passenger to film it, or setting up the video to do a selfie recording of themselves performing the stunt.

Some of the early versions had the cars moving at a really low speed. It seems now that some people have cars that crawl along at a much faster speed. It further seems that some people don't think about the dangers of this activity and they just "go for it" and figure that it will all work out fine and dandy. It often doesn't. Not surprising to most of us, I'd dare say.

The craze is referred to as either the Shiggy Challenge or the In My Feelings challenge (#InMyFeelings), and some more explicitly call it the moving car dance challenge. This craze has even got the feds involved. The National Transportation Safety Board (NTSB) issued a tweet that said this:" #OntheBlog we're sharing concerns about the #InMyFeelings challenge while driving. #DistractedDriving is dangerous and can be deadly. No call, no text, no update, and certainly no dance challenge is worth a human life."

Be forewarned that this antic can get you busted, including a distracted driving ticket, or worse still a reckless driving charge.

Now that I've told you about this wondrous and trending challenge, I want to emphasize that I only refer to it as an indicator of something otherwise worthy of discussion herein, namely the act of getting out of or into a moving car. I suppose it should go without stating that getting into a moving car is highly dangerous and discouraged. The second corollary equally valid would be that getting out of a moving car is highly dangerous and discouraged.

I'm sure someone will instantly retort that hey, Lance, there are times that it is necessary to get out of or into a moving car. Yes, I've seen the same spy movies as you, and I realize that when James Bond is in a moving car and being held at gun point, maybe the right spy action is to leap out of the car. Got it. Seriously, I'll be happy to concede that there are rare situations whereby getting into a moving car or out of a moving car might be needed, let's say the car is on fire and in motion or you are being kidnapped, there will be rare such moments. By-and-large, I would hope we all agree that those are rarities.

Sadly, there are annually a number of reported incidents of people getting run over by their own car. Somewhat recently, a person left their car engine running, they got out of the car to do something such as drop a piece of mail into a nearby mailbox, and the car inadvertently shifted into gear and ran them over. These oddities do happen from time to time. Again, extremely rare, but further illustrate the dangers of getting out of even a non-moving car for which the engine is running.

Prior to the advent of seat belts, and the gradual mandatory use and acceptance of seat belts in cars, there were a surprisingly sizable number of reported incidents of people "falling" out of their cars. Now, it could be that some of them jumped out while the car was moving and so it wasn't particularly the lack of a seat belt involved. On the other hand, there are documented cases of people sitting in a moving car, and not wearing a seat belt, while the car was in motion, and their car door open unexpectedly, with them then proceeding to accidentally hang outside of the car (often clinging to the door), or falling entirely out of the car onto the street.

This is why you should always wear your seat belt. Tip for the day.

For the daredevils of you, it might not be apparent why it is so bad to leave a moving car. If you are a passenger, you have a substantial chance of falling to the street and getting injured. Or, maybe you fall to the street and get killed by hitting the street with your head. Or, maybe you hit an object like a fire hydrant and get injured or killed. Or, maybe another car runs you over. Or, maybe the car you exited manages to drive over you. I think that paints the picture pretty well.

I'd guess that the human driver of the car might be shocked to have you suddenly leave the moving car. This could cause the human driver to make some kind of panic or erratic maneuver with the car. Thus, your "innocent" act of leaving the moving car could cause the human driver to swerve into another car, maybe injuring or killing other people.

Or, maybe you roll onto the ground and seem OK, but then the human driver turns the car to try and somehow catch you and actually hits you, injuring you or killing you. There are numerous acrobatic variations to this.

Suppose that it's the human driver that opts to leave the moving car? In that case, the car is now a torpedo ready to strike someone or something. It's an unguided missile. Sure, the car will likely start to slow down because the human driver is no longer pushing on the accelerator pedal, but depending upon the speed when the driver ejected, the multi-ton car still has a lot of momentum and chances of injuring or killing or hitting someone or something. If there are any human occupants inside the car, they too are now at the mercy of a car that is going without any direct driving direction.

Let's recap, you can exit from a moving car and these things could happen:

- You directly get injured (by say hitting the street)

- You directly get killed (by hitting the street with your head, let's say)

- You indirectly get injured (another car comes along and hits you)

- You indirectly get killed (the other car runs you over)

- Your action gets someone else injured (another car crashes trying to avoid you)

- Your action gets someone else killed (the other car rams a car and everyone gets killed)

I'm going to carve out a bit of an exception to this aspect of leaving a moving car. If you choose to leave the moving car or do so by happenstance, let's call that a "normal" exiting of a moving car. On the other hand, suppose the car gets into a car accident, unrelated for the moment to your exiting, and during the accident you are involuntarily thrown out of the car due to the car crash. That's kind of different than choosing to exit the moving car per se. Of course, this happens often when people that aren't wearing seat belts get into severe car crashes.

Anyway, let's consider that there's the bad news of exiting a moving car, and we also want to keep in mind that trying to get into a moving car has its own dangers too. I remember a friend of mine in college that opted to try jumping into the back passenger seat of a moving car (I believe some drinking had been taking place). His pal opened the back door, and urged him to jump in. He was lucky to have landed into the seat. He could have easily been struck by the moving car. He could have fallen to the street and gotten run over by the car. Again, injuries and potential death, for him, and for other occupants of the car, and for other nearby cars too.

I'd like to enlarge the list of moving car aspects to these:

- Exiting a moving car
- Entering a moving car
- Riding on a moving car
- Hanging onto a moving car
- Facing off with a moving car
- Chasing after a moving car
- Other

I've covered already the first two items, so let's consider the others on the list.

There are reports from time-to-time of people that opted to ride on the hood of a car, usually for fun, and unfortunately they fell off and got hurt or killed once the car got into motion.

Hanging onto a moving car was somewhat popularized by the "Back To The Future" movie series when Marty McFly (Michael J. Fox) opts to grab onto the back of a car while he's riding his skateboard. I'm not blaming the movie for this and realize it is something people already had done, but the movie did momentarily increase the popularity of trying this dangerous act.

Facing off with a moving car has sometimes been done by people that perhaps watch too many bull fights. They seem to think that they can hold a red cape and challenge the bull (the car). In my experience, the car is likely to win over the human standing in the street and facing off with the car. It's a weight thing.

Chasing after a moving car happens somewhat commonly in places like New York City. You see a cab, it fails to stop, you are in a hurry, so you run after the cab, yelling at the top of your lungs. With the advent of Uber and other ridesharing services, this doesn't happen as much as it used to. Instead, we let our mobile apps do our cab or rideshare hailing for us.

What does all of this have to do with AI self-driving cars?

At the Cybernetic AI Self-Driving Car Institute, we are developing AI software for self-driving cars, and one aspect that many auto makers and tech firms are not yet considering deals with the aforementioned things that people do regarding moving cars.

Some of the auto makers and tech firms would say that these various actions by humans, such as exiting a moving car or trying to get into a moving car, are considered an "edge" problem. An edge problem is one that is not at the core of the overarching problem being solved. If you are in the midst of trying to get AI to drive a car, you likely consider these cases of people exiting and entering a moving car to be such a remote possibility that you don't put much attention to it right now. You figure it's something to ultimately deal with, but getting the car to drive is foremost in your mind right now.

I've had some AI developers that tell me that if a human is stupid enough to exit from a moving car, they get what they deserve. Same for all of the other possibilities, such as trying to enter a moving car, chasing after a moving car, etc. The perspective is that the AI has enough to do already, and dealing with stupid human tricks (aka David Letterman!), that's just not very high priority. Humans do stupid things, and these AI developers shrug their shoulders and say that an

AI self-driving car is not going to ever be able to stop people from being stupid.

This narrow view by those AI developers is unfortunate.

I can already predict that there will be an AI self-driving car that while driving on the public roadways will have an occupant that opts to jump out of the moving self-driving car. Let's say that indeed this is a stupid act and the person had no particularly justifiable cause to do so. If the AI self-driving car proceeds along and does not realize that the person jumped out, and the AI blindly continues to drive ahead, I'll bet there will be backlash about this. Backlash against the particular self-driving car maker. Backlash against possibly the entire AI self-driving car industry. It could get ugly.

Let's take a moment and clarify too what is meant by an AI self-driving car. There are various levels of capabilities of AI self-driving cars. The topmost level is considered Level 5. A Level 5 AI self-driving car is one in which the AI is fully able to drive the car, and there is no requirement for a human driver to be present. Indeed, often a Level 5 self-driving car has no provision for human driving, encompassing that there aren't any pedals and not a steering wheel available for a human to use.

For self-driving cars less than a Level 5, it is expected that a human driver will be present and that the AI and the human driver will co-share the driving task. I've mentioned many times that this co-sharing arrangement allows for dangerous situations and adverse consequences.

The level of an AI self-driving car is a crucial consideration in this discussion about people leaping out of a moving self-driving car or taking other such actions.

Consider first the self-driving cars less than a Level 5. If the human driver that's supposed to be in the self-driving car is the one that jumps out, this leaves the AI alone to continue driving the car (assuming that no other human driver is an occupant and able to step into the human driving role of the co-sharing task). We likely don't want the AI to now be alone as the driver, since for levels less than 5 it is considered a precondition that there be a human driver present. As such, the AI needs to ascertain that the human driver is no longer present, and as a minimum proceed to take some concerted effort to safely bring the self-driving car to a proper and appropriate halt.

Would we want the AI in the less-than level 5 self-driving car to take any special steps about the exited human? This is somewhat of an open question because the expectation of what the AI can accomplish at the less-than level 5 is that it is not fully yet sophisticated. It could be that we might agree that at the less-than level 5, the most we can expect is that the AI will try to safely bring the self-driving car to a halt. It won't try to somehow go around and pick-up the person or take other actions that we would expect a human driver to possibly undertake.

This brings us to the Level 5 self-driving car. It too should be established to detect that someone has left the moving self-driving car. In this case, it doesn't matter whether the person that left is a driver or not, because no human driver is needed anyway. In that sense, in theory, the driving can continue. It's now a question of what to do about the human that left the moving car.

In essence, with the Level 5 self-driving car, we have more options of what to have the AI do in this circumstance. It could just ignore that a human abruptly left the car, and continue along, acting as though nothing happened at all. Or, it could have some kind of provision of action to take in such situations, and invoke that action. Or, it could act similar to the less-than Level 5 self-driving cars and merely seek to safely and appropriately bring the self-diving car to a halt.

One would question the approach of not doing anything and yet being aware that a human left the self-driving car while in motion, this seems counter intuitive to what we would expect or hope that the AI would do. If the AI is acting like a human driver, we would certainly expect that the human driver would do something overtly about the occupant that has left the moving car. Call 911. Slow down. Turn around. Do something. Unless the human driver and the occupants are somehow in agreement about leaving the self-driving car, and maybe they made some pact to do so, it would seem prudent and expected that a human driver would do something to come to the aid of the other person. Thus, so should the AI.

You might wonder how would the AI even realize that a human has left the car?

Consider that there are these key aspects of the driving task by the AI:

- Sensor data collection and interpretation
- Sensor fusion
- Virtual world model updating
- AI action planning
- Car controls commands issuance

The AI self-driving car will likely have sensors pointing outward of the car, such as the use of radar, cameras, LIDAR, sonar, and the like. These provide an indication of what is occurring outside of the self-driving car in the surrounding environment.

It is likely that there will also be sensors pointing inward into the car compartment. For example, it is anticipated that there will be cameras and an audio microphone in the car compartment. The microphone allows for the human occupants to verbally interact with the AI system, similar to interacting with a Siri or Alexa. The camera would allow those within the self-driving car to be seen, such as if the self-driving car is being used to drive your children to school that you could readily see that they are doing OK inside the AI self-driving car.

I'll walk you through a scenario of an AI self-driving car at a Level 5 and the case of someone that opts to exit from the self-driving car while it is in motion.

Joe and Samatha have opted to use the family AI self-driving car to go to the beach. They both gather up their beach towels and sunscreen, and get into the AI self-driving car. Joe tells the AI to take them to the beach. Dutifully, the AI system repeats back that it will head to the beach and indicates an estimated arrival time. Samatha and Joe settle into their seats and opt to watch a live video stream of a volleyball tournament taking place at the beach and for which they hope to arrive there before it ends.

At this juncture, the AI system would have used the inward facing camera to detect that two people are in the self-driving car. In fact, it would recognize them since it is the family car and they have been in it many times before. The AI sets the internal environment to their normal preferences, such as the temperature, the lighting, and the rest. It proceeds to drive the car to the beach.

Once the self-driving car gets close to the beach, turns out there's lots of traffic as many other people opted to drive to the beach that day. Joe starts to get worried that he's going to miss seeing the end of the volleyball game in-person. So, while the self-driving car is crawling along at about five to eight miles per hour in solid traffic, Joe suddenly decides to open the car door and leap out. He then runs over to the volleyball game to see the last few moments of the match.

The AI system would have detected that the car door had opened and closed. The inward facing cameras would have detected that Joe had moved toward the door and exited the door. The outward facing cameras, the sonar, the radar, and the LIDAR would all have detected him once he got out of the self-driving car. The sensor fusion would have put together the data from those outward facing sensors have been able to ascertain that a human was near to the self-driving car, and proceeding away from the self-driving car at a relatively fast pace.

The virtual world model would have contained an indicator of a human near to the self-driving car, once Joe had gotten out of the self-driving car. And, it would also have indicators of the other nearby cars.

It is plausible then that the AI would via the sensors be aware that Joe had been in the self-driving car, had gotten out of it, and was then moving away from it.

The big question then is what should the AI action planning do? If Joe's exit does not pose a threat to the AI self-driving car, in the sense that Joe moved rapidly away from it, and so he's not a potential inadvertent target of the self-driving car by its moving forward, presumably there's not much that needs to be done. The AI doesn't need to slow down or stop the car. But, this is unclear since it could be that Joe somehow fell out of the car, and so maybe the self-driving car should come to a halt safely.

Here's where the interaction part comes to play. The AI could potentially ask the remaining human occupant, Samantha, about what has happened and what to do. It could have even called out to Joe, when he first opened the door to exit, and asked what he's doing. Joe, had he been thoughtful, could have even beforehand told the AI that he was planning on jumping out of the car while it is in motion, and thus a kind of "pact" would have been established.

These aspects are not so easily decided upon. Suppose the human occupant is unable to interact with the AI, or refuses to do so? This is a contingency that the AI needs to contend with. Suppose the human is purposely doing something highly dangerous? Perhaps in this case that when Joe jumped out, there was another car coming up that the AI could detect and knew might hit Joe, what should the AI have done?

Some say that maybe the best way to deal with this aspect of leaping out of the car involves forcing the car doors to be unable to be opened by the human occupants when inside the AI self-driving car. This might seem appealing, as an easy answer, but it fails to recognize the complexity of the real-world. Will people accept the idea that they are locked inside an AI self-driving car and cannot get out on their own?

Doubtful. If you say that just have the humans tell the AI to unlock the door when they want to get out, and the AI can refuse when the car is in motion, this again will likely be met with skepticism by humans as a viable means of human control over the automation.

A similar question though does exist about self-driving cars and children.

If AI self-driving cars are going to be used to send your children to school or play, do you want those children to be able to get out of the self-driving car whenever they wish? Probably not. You would want the children to be forced to stay inside. But, there's no adult present to help determine when unlocking the doors is good or not to do. Some say that by having inward facing cameras and a Skype like feature, the parents could be the ones that instruct the AI via live streaming to go ahead and unlock the doors when appropriate. This of course has downsides since it makes the assumption that there will be a responsible adult available for this purpose and that they'll have a real-time connection to the self-driving car, etc.

Each of the other actions by humans such as entering the car while in-motion, chasing after a self-driving car, hanging onto a self-driving car, riding on top of a self-driving car, and so on, they all have their own particulars as to what the AI should and maybe should not do.

Being able to detect any of these human actions is the "easier" part since it involves finding objects and tracking those objects (when I say easy, I am not saying that the sensors will work flawlessly and nor that it can necessarily reliably make such detections, I am simply saying that the programming for this is clearer than the AI action planning is).

Using machine learning or similar kinds of automation for figuring out what to do is unlikely as a means of getting out of the pickle of what the AI should do. There are generally few instances of these kind, and each instance would tend to have its own unique circumstances. It would be hard to have a large enough training set. There would also be the concern that the learning would overfit to the limited data and thus not be viable in generalizable situations that are likely to arise.

Our view of this is that it is something requiring templates and programmatic solutions, rather than an artificial neural network or similar. Nonetheless, allow me to emphasize that we still see these as circumstances that once encountered should go up to the cloud of the AI system for purposes of sharing with the rest of the system and for enhancing the abilities of the on-board AI systems that otherwise have not yet encountered such instances.

The odds are high that human occupants will be tempted to jump out of a moving AI self-driving car more so than a human driven car, or similarly try to get into one that is moving. I say this because at first, humans will likely be timid with the AI and be hesitant to do anything untoward, but after a while the AI will become more accepted and humans will become bolder. If your friend or parent is driving the car, you are likely more socially bound to not do strange tricks, you would worry that they might get in trouble. With the AI driving the car, you have no such social binding per se. I'm sure that many maverick teenagers will delight in "tricking" the AI self-driving car into doing all sorts of Instagram worthy untoward things.

Of course, it's not always just maverick kinds of actions that would occur. I've had situations wherein I was driving in an area that was unfamiliar, and a friend walked ahead of my car, guiding the way. If you owned an AI self-driving car of Level 5, you might want it to do the same -- you get out of the self-driving car and have it follow you. In theory, the self-driving car should come to a stop before you get out, and likewise be stopped when you want to get in, but is this always going to be true? Do we want to have such unmalleable rules for our AI self-driving cars?

Should your AI self-driving car enable you to undertake the Shiggy Challenge?

In theory, a Level 5 AI self-driving car could do so and even help you do so. It could do the video recording of your dancing. It could respond to your verbal commands to slow down or speed-up the car. It could make sure to avoid any upcoming cars and thus avert the possibility of ramming into someone else while you are dancing wildly to "In My Feelings." This is relatively straightforward.

But, as a society, do we want this to be happening? Will it encourage behavior that ultimately is likely to lead to human injury and possibly death? We can add this to a long list of the ethics aspects of AI self-driving cars. Meanwhile, it's something that cannot be neglected, else we'll for sure have AI that's unaware and those "stupid" humans will get themselves into trouble and the AI might get axed because of it.

As the song says: "Gotta be real with it, yup."

CHAPTER 12
SPORTS CARS
AND
AI SELF-DRIVING CARS

CHAPTER 12

SPORTS CARS
AND AI SELF-DRIVING CARS

Aha, the joys of driving a sports car! You feel the sports car hugging the road and the nimble handling allows you to sweetly make those tight turns. With impeccable steering, amazing aerodynamics, superb suspension, high maneuverability, and spirited performance, you are in your own dream world while actually rocketing down the open highway at a cruising speed of 120 miles per hour, doing so knowing that your sports car tops out at 200 mph and you've got a lot zip yet to be applied on your speedometer.

Maybe you are driving a Ford Shelby GT350 that can hit 180 mph, goes from 0 to 60 mph in 3.7 seconds and has a horsepower of 526. Or, maybe instead you opted for the Dodge SRT Viper which can top out at 206 mph, does the 0 to 60 mph in just 2.3 seconds and has a horsepower of 645. Or, perhaps you wanted to put your other sports cars pals to shame, so you shelled out the big bucks to get yourself a Hennessey Venom, allowing you to hit speeds of up to 270 and having a horsepower of a whopping 1244.

Some people get a sports car because they like the speed, the handling, and the other features that allow for a special driving experience. Some get a sports car because they love the image of a sports car, and a sports car driver, often seen as someone that relishes the open road, a maverick, and that craves the looks of other people as they turn their heads to see what that sports car is (and who's in it). You could also suggest that a sports car could be an investment, though you'd need to keep it in good shape. But, nonetheless, yes, many "hobbyists" collect sports cars like you might collect stamps. Sometimes those collectors don't even drive the sports cars and merely put them on display at their man cave or woman cave.

When someone drives a sports car, they can do so on our public roadways or drive it on private so-called closed tracks.

In theory, when you drive a sports car on a public roadway, you are supposed to abide by the driving laws. If you are driving on an open highway and the speed limit is say 75 mph, you aren't supposed to be going 180 mph, even if your sports car can do so. I've had some sports car owners that tell me they couldn't help but go way over the speed limit since the sports car is so quiet at 150 mph they had no idea they had doubled the speed limit. The sports car is purring at those speeds, they say.

Nonetheless, the law is the law. It doesn't really matter that you happen to have a sports car. The speed limit is the same for a junkie jalopy as it is for the souped-up sports car. Most police usually have little sympathy for the sports car driver caught going at an outrageous speed, or doing swerving tactics that maybe befit a sports car but that can anyway be considered a hazard to traffic.

By-and-large, sports car drivers seem to end-up in one of three camps for portions of their driving time:
- Legal
- Quasi-legal
- Illegal

The legal driving is usually when they sense that there's a cop nearby, or when they are jammed-up in bumper to bumper traffic, or otherwise not in a viable situation to do anything other than pure legal driving.

The quasi-legal camp will push every law to the limit, whenever possible. That off-ramp up ahead has a posted speed of 45 mph and is trying to advise drivers to watch out for the curve that might force your car off the road and into a ditch if you are going too fast. That's really just a "challenge me" sign for the sports car driver. They want to see how much their tires will squeal and the car will flow thunderously into the curve, vastly exceeding the recommended speed and the driver betting that no police will stop them for such a potential infraction.

The illegal camp goes beyond the limits of the law. They are hopeful they won't get caught. You've seen these drivers. They will try to stay out of the fast lane under the belief that it makes them an easier to see target by the police. Thus, they will go at high speeds in the slower lanes, figuring that the other cars they are nearly side swiping are acting as a kind of radar defensive shield. At every opportunity, they will blatantly break the law. Some do it without a care in the world and are flagrant as they do so. Others try to hide it and pretend that nobody official will notice their transgressions.

For those that want to push their sports car to the limits, there are places they can do so without putting the rest of the public in jeopardy. Here in Southern California, we recently had a Porsche Experience Center open up. It provides a 53-acre fun park for Porsche drivers. There's a road handling course, and its only one of five worldwide that Porsche has established. Besides various road surfaces, there's an Ice Hill which has a 7% slope that jets of water can soak down to make for a low friction surface, and they have a Kick Plate that is intended to induce a skid or spin, etc.

Admittedly, these closed course tracks are nice, but there are too few of them to be within easy access of all sports car owners, plus they often are for certain brands only, and worst of all for many sports car drivers it just isn't fully as satisfying as going on the public roadways. Going around and around in circles on a few miles long track is not the same as driving for dozens or hundreds of miles in your sports car. Some might also find that there's a thrill of getting caught, which isn't the case when driving on a closed track (usually, instead, it's the "thrill" of guiding the sports car close into a death defying stunt).

Some people hate sports cars and sports car drivers. Those pesky and annoying sports car drivers think they are high and mighty. They think they can squeeze in and out of traffic wherever they wish. Egoistical. Maniac drivers. Scofflaws. Even regulators at times will clamp down hard on sports cars. An extra tax or fee can be a means to get some added dough out of those sports car owners that just must have their sports cars. When the sports car owners complain, they are told they should be happy that they still get a chance to driver their vaunted vehicles on our roads.

The emotional relationship between a sports car owner and their sports car can be as strong as say the personal ties between a dog owner and their pet dog. You've maybe seen a sports car owner that talks to their sports car. They might meticulously clean their sports car. They keep it parked inside or perhaps have a special cover for their sports car. When they start the sports car, they let the engine rev up. Upon entering into an area that has lots of sharp pebbles, they will drive the car at exceedingly slow speeds to keep the rocks from bouncing up to scratch the paint job. Tender. Loving. Care.

What does this have to do with AI self-driving cars?

At the Cybernetic AI Self-Driving Car Institute, we are developing AI software for self-driving cars, and as part of that effort we're also considering the role of sports cars in a future consisting of AI self-driving cars.

Let's then consider what the future holds for sports cars.

There are some AI self-driving car pundits that are saying we'll eventually have only and all AI self-driving cars on our roadways. This nirvana will allow somehow that all traffic snarls of today to disappear, because presumably the AI self-driving cars will either all communicate with each other via V2V (vehicle to vehicle communication) or V2I (vehicle to infrastructure communication), and coordinate their movement. This will be done either by a master governmental traffic flow system, or by a negotiated peer-to-peer kind of approach.

Before I further consider the aforementioned scenario, please be aware that it is not going to be overnight that we suddenly find ourselves with exclusively AI self-driving cars on our roadways. There are an estimated 200+ million conventional cars today in the United States alone. Those are not going to miraculously turn into AI self-driving cars. It will be many years before we do away with all of those conventional cars. Thus, the nirvana envisioned by some pundits is eons away in time and I'd say let's not get ourselves too far ahead of the game about this.

But, suppose we did live in a world of only AI self-driving cars on our roadways. What does that signify for the sports car? If you believe that AI self-driving cars will only be permitted to drive in a fully legal manner, it means that those sports car owners aren't going to be able to drive in a quasi-legal manner anymore and for sure not in an illegal manner. Ouch, that hurts for those sports car lovers. It cuts out a chunk of the joy of having a sports car.

Well, maybe that aspect of being forced into legal driving mode will only apply if you are on the public roadways. Would we as a society allow for the AI self-driving sports car to be able to drive "illegally" if it is on closed track that is outside the purview of the public roadways? You would certainly think this would be a reasonable desire by sports car owners. Look, they might say, I'll have my AI self-driving sports car drive legally when on public roads, but when not on public roads the sky is the limit.

Some might argue that this is bound to be a recipe for disaster. Suppose the AI self-driving sports car somehow gets into sports driving mode while on a public roadway? How would we police this aspect to prevent the AI self-driving sports cars from doing so? Maybe a sports car owner could hack their sports car to allow them to make it go into a sports car driving mode whenever they wished to do so. I am guessing there will be some opponents of sports car driving that will insist that no AI system can ever drive a car as though it is a sports car. In essence, prevent the capability to even exist, and then you remove the chances of anyone abusing the capability.

Will we have sports car owners that say you'll remove their sports driving feature only over their dead body and after you've pried their cold- hardened hands off the steely grip of the sporty steering wheel?

Maybe.

Continuing for a moment the perspective of an AI self-driving car only world, there's another angle on the sports car aspects. Suppose we do have some master control or maybe a peer-to-peer coordination system for traffic control. One approach to sports cars might be to charge them a special fee to be able to use their sports car driving mode.

You can bring your AI self-driving sports car onto the freeway, and let's say in the mornings when there's a lot of traffic, your sports driving mode must be disabled. But, in the afternoon, when there is open traffic, you can make use of the sports driving mode, but only to the extent allowed by the master control system or the peer-to-peer coordinating system. You can do this for an extra charge. You must pay the public for being allowed to do so. This could raise lots of money for other public causes, whether it be to keep our roadway infrastructure updated or for the homeless or other such causes.

Maybe sports car owners would find this acceptable and sufficient. Some might be upset that they can't use their sports car driving mode whenever they want. There might be the public at large that sees this as an elitist kind of thing and though the sports car owner has to pay for privilege, it seems like only the privileged are going to be able to do so. This will be a societal debate, certainly.

We need to clarify in this discussion what is meant by an AI self-driving car. There are various levels of AI self-driving cars. The topmost level, a Level 5, consists of an AI self-driving car that has no human driver. The AI is intended to be the driver. Indeed, there is usually no provision for a human driver in a Level 5 self-driving car, including that there aren't any pedals and there isn't a steering wheel. For self-driving cars less than a Level 5, the self-driving car must contain a licensed human driver, and the human driver and the AI are co-sharing the driving task. This is something that provides numerous worrisome concerns.

In the nirvana world of all AI self-driving cars, they are envisioned as all and only the Level 5 self-driving cars.

What about a world in which there are a mixture of conventional cars being driven by humans, and AI self-driving cars "less than" level 5 that are therefore co-sharing the driving task with humans, and the AI self-driving cars of a Level 5 that are being driven only by the AI?

Let's consider the sports car aspect in that scenario, which is actually the more realistic scenario.

As an aside, for a long time, we're going to have a mixture just like the aforementioned. At first, there will be very few of the Level 5's, there will be lots of the conventional cars, and some of the "less than" Level 5's. Over many years, the mixture will gradually shift such that there will be less and less conventional cars, and more and more of the "less than" Level 5 self-driving cars, and a rising amount of Level 5 self-driving cars. The nirvana world will arrive, if it does, once that mixture becomes purely just Level 5 self-driving cars.

Well, in any case, you get onto the freeway and suppose you see some sports cars that are conventional sports cars and driven only by humans. And, you also see some advanced sports cars that are AI self-driving cars but at the "less than" Level 5, and so those sports cars are at times being driven by the AI and at other times being driven by the human. Plus, you see some advanced sports cars that are pure Level 5 and so only the AI is actually driving those sports cars.

Would it make sense to restrict the Level 5's from not driving in a sports car driving kind of way? If you do so, why then are you allowing the conventional sports car to be driven by a human in a sports car driving way, and the same for the instance of the "less than" Level 5? In other words, it seems like either they all get to drive as though they are driving a sports car, or none of them should.

I realize you might say that the Level 5 shouldn't be able to drive in a sports car driving mode because it's AI and not a human. But, this suggests a distrust that the AI cannot drive as well as a human can. If that's the case, then the Level 5 self-driving car probably shouldn't even be on the road. In other words, the AI should be able to drive an AI self-driving sports car, otherwise that vehicle shouldn't be on the public roadways to begin with.

Which brings us to another key point, namely, many of the auto makers and tech firms are right now focusing on getting the AI to drive a self-driving car in its most rudimentary driving means. Thus, the AI won't necessarily be able to leverage any special capabilities of the car itself. Thus, if you have a sports car that has this kind of AI, it likely won't be able to take advantage naturally of the sports car speed, maneuverability, etc.

Some consider this to be a so-called "edge" problem. An edge problem is considered something that is not at the core of the problem that you are trying to solve. In the case of cars, the core problem in the view of many AI developers is to be able to have the AI drive a car in the most simplistic way possible, as though an average adult driver was driving the car. For a sports car, sure an average adult driver can drive it, but if you want to drive it well, and really exercise what it can do, you need to have "above average" driving skills or at least somewhat more specialized driving skills.

That's what we are working on – developing the AI software for solving the edge problem of being able to drive a sports car as it was meant to be driven.

Let's now then revisit our earlier mixture of cars that are on the freeway. Suppose we have conventional sports cars with human drivers, we have sports cars co-sharing driving of the humans with the AI "less than" Level 5's, and we've got sports cars with the Level 5's. Assume that the AI's are all versed in sports car driving. Do we allow sport car driving to occur or do we not?

We'd likely assume that the human drivers are going to do their usual legal/quasi-legal/illegal sports driving, doing so with their conventional sports cars.

The co-sharing driving creates a conundrum because we might have the AI that opts to drive like a sports car driver, but for which gets into a pickle and suddenly hands over the driving to the human driver, but perhaps the human driver at that point is not versed in sports car driving and cannot then deal with whatever dire situation has arisen. Or, likewise, the human driver has gotten the sports car into a pickle and wants the AI to take over control, but the AI doesn't know what to do given that the pickle is underway.

The Level 5 would almost seem like the better choice at being able to then drive the sports car, assuming that it is versed in doing so, since you've removed the co-sharing confusion, and you've removed the human driver entirely. That being said, what joy remains for the human occupant that is in the sports car of a Level 5?

I began this discussion by pointing out the various reasons that humans seem to love their sports cars. If it's a Level 5 self-driving sports car, and you the human have nothing to do with the actual driving, does that drain the joy from being in the sports car? And, furthermore, if there are restrictions on when the sports car driving mode can actually be employed, will that further diminish the joy? Perhaps, sports cars will no longer have much interest and therefore the only sports cars made will be either for competitive racing purposes or for collectors to put on display like in a museum. Will society as a whole gradually lose its sense of image of what a sports car represents? Maybe over time, this whole maverick thing and the other attributes of owning and driving a sports car will wane.

Some say that people will always relish sports cars. It's in our blood. Furthermore, what better way to experience a sports car than by having an expert-level race car driver that will be your electronic chauffeur whenever you wish, 24 hours per day and 7 days per week.

Some of the sports car makers at first insisted they would never make a fully autonomous sports car, but have tended to back-down when they realized that in a future economy of ridesharing, wherein perhaps people don't buy cars anymore, and use AI Level 5 self-driving cars as their primary means to get around, if there aren't Level 5 sports cars then there's nothing left but crumbs for the sports car makers. Better to join the Level 5 club, than to be on the outside looking in. Well, however this works out, I think there's one credo that many of us will always have: I feel the need, the need for speed. Go out and take your sports car for a spin, while you can.

CHAPTER 13

GAME THEORY

AND AI SELF-DRIVING CARS

CHAPTER 13

GAME THEORY

AND AI SELF-DRIVING CARS

When you get onto the freeway, you are essentially entering into the matrix. For those of you familiar with the movie of the same name, you'll realize that I am suggesting that you are entering into a kind of simulated world as your car proceeds up the freeway onramp and into the flow of traffic. Whether you know it or not, you are indeed opting into playing a game, though one much more serious than an amusement park bumper cars arena.

On the freeway, you are playing a game of life-and-death. It might seem like you are merely driving to work or trying to get to the ballgame, but the reality is that for every moment you are on the freeway you are at risk of your life. Your car can go awry, say it suddenly loses a tire, and you swerve across the lanes, possibly ramming into other cars or going off a freeway embankment. Or, you might be driving perfectly well, and all of a sudden, a truck ahead of you unexpectedly slams on its breaks and you crash into the truck.

I hope this doesn't seem morbid. Nor do I want to appear to be an alarmist. But, you have to admit, these scenarios are all possible and you are in fact at the risk of your life while on the freeway. For a novice driver, such as a teenager starting to drive, you can usually see on their face an expression that sums up the freeway driving circumstance – abject fear. They know that one wrong move can be fatal. They are usually somewhat surprised that anyone would trust a teenager to be in such a situation of great responsibility. Most teenagers are held in contempt by adults for a lack of taking responsibility seriously, and yet we let them get behind the wheel of a multi-ton car and drive amongst the rest of us.

That's not to suggest that its only teenage drivers that understand this matter. There are many everyday drivers that know how serious being on the freeway is. They grip the steering wheel with both hands and arch their backs and are paying close attention to every moment while on the freeway. Meanwhile, there are drivers that have gotten so used to driving on the freeway that they act as though they are at a bumper car ride and don't care whether they cut off other drivers or nearly cause accidents. They zoom along and seem to not have a care in the world. One always wonders whether those drivers are the ones that get into the accidents that you see while on the freeway. Are they more prone to accidents or are they actually more able to skirt around accidents, which maybe they indirectly caused, but managed to avoid themselves getting entangled into.

Anyway, if you are willing to concede that we can think of freeway driving as a game, you then might be also willing to accept the idea that we can potentially use game theory to help understand and model driving behavior.

With game theory, we can consider the freeway driving and the traffic to be something that can be mathematically modeled. This mathematical model can take into account conflict. A car cuts off another car. One car is desperately trying to get ahead of another car. And so on. The mathematical model can also take into account cooperation. As you enter onto the freeway, perhaps other cars let you in by purposely slowing down and making an open space for you. Or, you are in the fast lane and want to get over to the slow lane, so you turn on your blinker and other cars let you make your way from one lane to the next. There is at times cooperative behavior on the freeway, and likewise at times there is behavior involving conflict.

If this topic generally interests you, there's key work by John Glen Wardrop that produced what is considered the core principles of equilibrium in traffic assignment. Traffic assignment is the formal name given to modeling traffic situations. He developed mathematical models that showcase how we seek to minimize our cost of travel, and that we potentially can reach various points of equilibrium in doing so. At times, traffic suffers and can be modeled as doing so due to the "price of anarchy," which is based on presumably selfish oriented behavior.

For those of you that are into computer science, you likely are familiar with the work of John von Neumann. Of his many contributions to the field of computing and mathematics, he's also known for his work involving zero-sum games. Indeed, he made use of Brouwer's fixed-point theorem in topology, and had observed that when you dissolve sugar in a cup of coffee that there's always a point without motion. We'll come back to this later on in this exploration of game theory and freeway traffic.

Let's first define what a zero-sum game consists of. In a zero-sum game, the choices by the players will not decrease and nor increase the amount of available resources, and thus they are competing against a bounded set of resources. Each player wants their piece of the pie, and in so doing are keeping that piece away from the other player. The pie is not going to expand or contract, it stays the same size. Meanwhile, the players are fighting over the slices and when someone else takes a slice it means there's one less for the other players to have. A non-zero sum game allows for the pie to be increased and thus one player doesn't necessarily benefit at the expense of the other players.

When you are on the freeway, you at times experience a zero-sum game, while at other times it is a non-zero sum game. Suppose you come upon a bunch of stopped traffic up ahead of you. You realize that there's an accident and it has led to the traffic halting. You are going to get stuck behind the traffic and be late to work. Looking around, you see that there's a freeway offramp that you could use to get off the freeway and take side streets to get around the snarl.

It turns out that the freeway traffic is slowly moving forward up toward the blockage, and meanwhile other cars are also realizing that maybe they should try to get to the offramp. You are in the fast lane, which is the furthest lane from the exit ramp. The cars in the other closer lanes are all vying to make the exit. They don't care about you. They care about themselves making the exit. If they were to let you into their lane, it would increase your chances of getting to the offramp, but simultaneously decrease their chances. This is due to the aspect that the traffic is slowly moving forward and will gradually push past the offramp. There's a short time window involved and it's a dog eat dog situation. Zero-sum game.

But suppose instead the situation involved all the cars that were behind the snarl to share with each other to get to the offramp. Politely and with civility, the cars each allowed other cars around them to make the offramp. Furthermore, there was an emergency lane that the cars opted to use, which otherwise wasn't supposed to be used, and opened up more available resources to allow the traffic to flow over to the exit. Non-zero sum game (of sorts).

Game theory attempts to use applied mathematics to model the behavior of humans and animals, and in so doing explain how games are played. This can be done in a purely descriptive manner, meaning that game theory will only describe what is going on about a game. This can also be done in a prescriptive manner, meaning that game theory can advise about what should be done when playing a game.

What does this have to do with AI self-driving cars?

At the Cybernetic AI Self-Driving Car Institute, we are using game theory to aid in modeling the traffic that will occur with the advent of AI self-driving cars.

There are some that believe in a nirvana world whereby all cars on the roadways will be exclusively AI self-driving cars. This provides a grand opportunity to essentially control all cars and do so in a macroscopic manner. Presumably, either by government efforts or by other means, we could setup some master system that would direct the traffic on our roads. Imagine that when you got onto the freeway, all of the cars on the freeway were under the control of a master traffic flow system. Each car was to obey strictly to the master traffic flow system. It alone would determine which lane each car would be in, what the speed of the car would be, when it will change lanes, etc.

In this scenario, it is assumed that there would never be traffic snarls again. Somehow the master traffic flow system would prevent traffic snarls from occurring. All traffic would magically flow along at maximum speeds and we could increase the speed limit to say 120 miles per hour. Pretty exciting!

But, this is something that seems less based on mathematics and more so based on a hunch and a dream.

It's also somewhat hard to believe that humans are going to be willing to give up the control of their cars to a master traffic flow system. I realize you might immediately point out that if people are willing to secede control of the driving task to an AI-based self-driving car, it's a simple next step to then secede that their particular AI self-driving car must obey some master traffic control system. We'll have to wait and see whether people will want their AI self-driving car to be an individualized driver, or whether they'll be accepting that their individualized driver will become a robot Borg of the larger collective.

Anyway, even if all of this is interesting to postulate, it still omits the real-world aspect that we are not going to have all and only AI self-driving cars for a very long time. In the United States alone, there are 200+ million conventional cars. Those conventional cars are not going to disappear overnight and be replaced with AI self-driving cars. It's just not economically feasible. As such, we're going to have a mixture of AI self-driving cars and conventional cars for quite some time.

Let's make that even longer too, due to the aspect that there are different levels of AI self-driving cars. A true self-driving car is considered at Level 5. That's a self-driving car for which the AI does all of the driving. There is no need for a human driver. There is indeed usually no provision for a human driver, and the driving controls such as the steering wheel and pedals are not even present. For self-driving cars less than Level 5, the driving task is co-shared between the human driver and the AI.

We might as well then say that the self-driving cars that are less than a Level 5 are pretty much in the same boat as the conventional cars. This is due to the aspect that the human driver can still take over the driving task. If we have even one ounce of human driving, we're back to the situation that it's going to be problematic to have a master traffic flow system that commands all cars to obey. You might argue that maybe when a less than level 5 self-driving car gets onto the freeway we could jury rig those cars to obey the master traffic flow system, but this seems like a credibility stretch of how this would play out.

You could even stand this topic on its ear by making the following proposal. Forget about AI self-driving cars per se. Instead, let's make all cars to have some kind of remote car driving capability. We add this into all cars, conventional or otherwise. When any car gets onto the freeway, it must have this remote control feature included, otherwise it is banned from getting onto the freeway. So, we've now reduced all such cars to follow-along automata that the master traffic flow system can control. We would somehow lock-out the human driving controls and only allow the use of the remote control, during the time that the car is on the freeway.

If we did this, it might give us the nirvana traffic flow advantages that some claim they see in the future. And it would still allow for human driving, but just not on the freeways, or maybe only on the freeways at off-hours and that during the morning traffic and evening traffic times the master flow system takes over all such cars on the freeways. We then wouldn't need to be in a rush to perfect the AI self-driving cars, since instead we've just outfitted cars with this remote control feature. It would be a lot easier than trying to get a car to drive like a human does, which is what the AI self-driving car efforts are trying to achieve.

Well, I really doubt we'll have us all accept the notion of having a remote control driving feature placed into our conventional cars. This seems like something that society at large would have severe heartburn over. It has too much of a Big Brother smell to it.

That's actually why so far there seems to be such overall support for AI self-driving cars. Most people tend to assume that an AI self-driving car will obey whomever the human occupant is. It's like having your own electronic chauffeur that is always at your beck and call. If instead it was being pitched that AI self-driving cars would allow for governmental control of all car traffic and that wherever you wanted your AI self-driving car to go would first need to be cleared by the government, I'd bet we'd have a lot of people saying let's put the brakes on this AI self-driving car thing.

Now, it could be that we at first have AI self-driving cars that are all about individual needs. You are able to use your AI self-driving car to drive you wherever you want to go, and however you want to get there. But, then there's a gradual realization that it might be prudent to collective guide those AI self-driving cars. And so via V2I (vehicle to infrastructure) communication, we creep down that path by having the roads tell your AI self-driving car which road to take and how fast to go. This then expands and eventually reaches a point whereby all AI self-driving cars are doing this. The next step becomes master control. Ouch, we got back to that. It's just that it might happen by happenstance over time, rather than as part of a large-scale master plan.

Returning to the aspect about using game theory, we can at least try to do traffic simulations and attempt to see what might happen as more and more cars become AI self-driving cars, especially those that are at the vaunted Level 5.

These simulations use various payoff matrices to gauge what will happen as an AI self-driving car drives alongside human driven cars. A symmetric payoff is one that depends upon the strategy being deployed and not the AI or person deploying it, while an asymmetric payoff is dependent. We also include varying degrees of cooperative behavior versus non-cooperative behavior.

John Nash made some crucial contributions to game theory and ultimately was awarded the Nobel Prize in Economic Science for it. His mathematical formulation suggested that when there are two or more players in a game, at some point there will be an equilibrium state such that no player can do any better than they are already doing. The sad thing is that we cannot yet predict per se when that equilibrium point is going to be reached – well, let's say it is very hard to do. This is still an open research problem and if you can solve it, good for you, and it might get you your very own Nobel Prize too.

Why would we want to be able to predict that point of equilibrium? Because we could then potentially guide the players toward it. On the freeway, imagine that you have a hundred cars all moving along. Some are not doing so well and are behind in terms of trying to get to work on time. Others are doing really well and ahead of schedule and will get to work with plenty of time to spare. All else being equal, if we had a master traffic flow system, suppose it could reposition and guide the cars so that they would all be at their best possible state.

But if we aren't able to figure out that best possible state, there's no means to therefore guide everyone toward it. We instead have to use a hit-and-miss approach (not literally hit, just metaphorically). In more formal terms, Nash stated that for a game of a finite number of moves, there exists a means by which the player can randomly choose their moves such that they will ultimately reach a collective point of equilibrium, and that at that point no player can further improve their situation.

You might say that everyone has reached the happiest point to which they can arrive, given the status of everyone else involved too. When I earlier said it was hard to calculate the point of equilibrium, I was suggesting that it can be found but that it is computationally expensive to do so. Some of you might be familiar with classes of mathematical problems that are considered computable in polynomial time (P), and others that are NP (non-deterministic polynomial time). We aren't sure yet whether the calculation of Nash's point of equilibrium is P or NP. Right now, it seems hard to calculate, that we can say for sure.

By the way, for those of you looking for a Nobel Prize, please let us know if $P = NP$.

Game theory will increasingly become important to designing and shaping traffic flow on our roads, particularly once we begin to see the advent of true Level 5 AI self-driving cars. The effort to mathematically model conflict and cooperation in our traffic will involve not only the intelligent rational human decision makers, along with their irrational behavior, but also the potential intelligent rational (and maybe irrational) behavior of the AI of the self-driving cars.

Getting a handle on the traffic aspects will allow AI developers to better shape the AI of the self-driving cars and will aid regulators and the public at large in experiencing what hopefully will be better traffic conditions than with human-only drivers. I don't think we want to end-up with AI self-driving cars that drive like those crazy human drivers that seem to not realize they are involved in a game of life-and-death. It's deadly out there and we need to make sure that the AI self-driving cars know how to best play that serious and somber game

APPENDIX

Lance B. Eliot

APPENDIX A

TEACHING WITH THIS MATERIAL

The material in this book can be readily used either as a supplemental to other content for a class, or it can also be used as a core set of textbook material for a specialized class. Classes where this material is most likely used include any classes at the college or university level that want to augment the class by offering thought provoking and educational essays about AI and self-driving cars.

In particular, here are some aspects for class use:

o   Computer Science. Studying AI, autonomous vehicles, etc.

o   Business. Exploring technology and it adoption for business.

o   Sociology. Sociological views on the adoption and advancement of technology.

Specialized classes at the undergraduate and graduate level can also make use of this material.

For each chapter, consider whether you think the chapter provides material relevant to your course topic. There is plenty of opportunity to get the students thinking about the topic and force them to decide whether they agree or disagree with the points offered and positions taken. I would also encourage you to have the students do additional research beyond the chapter material presented (I provide next some suggested assignments they can do).

RESEARCH ASSIGNMENTS ON THESE TOPICS

Your students can find background material on these topics, doing so in various business and technical publications. I list below the top ranked AI related journals. For business publications, I would suggest the usual culprits such as the Harvard Business Review, Forbes, Fortune, WSJ, and the like.

Here are some suggestions of homework or projects that you could assign to students:

a) <u>Assignment for foundational AI research topic</u>: Research and prepare a paper and a presentation on a specific aspect of Deep AI, Machine Learning, ANN, etc. The paper should cite at least 3 reputable sources. Compare and contrast to what has been stated in this book.

b) <u>Assignment for the Self-Driving Car topic</u>: Research and prepare a paper and Self-Driving Cars. Cite at least 3 reputable sources and analyze the characterizations. Compare and contrast to what has been stated in this book.

c) <u>Assignment for a Business topic</u>: Research and prepare a paper and a presentation on businesses and advanced technology. What is hot, and what is not? Cite at least 3 reputable sources. Compare and contrast to the depictions in this book.

d) <u>Assignment to do a Startup:</u> Have the students prepare a paper about how they might startup a business in this realm. They must submit a sound Business Plan for the startup. They could also be asked to present their Business Plan and so should also have a presentation deck to coincide with it.

You can certainly adjust the aforementioned assignments to fit to your particular needs and the class structure. You'll notice that I ask for 3 reputable cited sources for the paper writing based assignments. I usually steer students toward "reputable" publications, since otherwise they will cite some oddball source that has no credentials other than that they happened to write something and post it onto the Internet. You can define "reputable" in whatever way you prefer, for example some faculty think Wikipedia is not reputable while others believe it is reputable and allow students to cite it.

The reason that I usually ask for at least 3 citations is that if the student only does one or two citations they usually settle on whatever they happened to find the fastest. By requiring three citations, it usually seems to force them to look around, explore, and end-up probably finding five or more, and then whittling it down to 3 that they will actually use.

I have not specified the length of their papers, and leave that to you to tell the students what you prefer. For each of those assignments, you could end-up with a short one to two pager, or you could do a dissertation length paper. Base the length on whatever best fits for your class, and the credit amount of the assignment within the context of the other grading metrics you'll be using for the class.

I mention in the assignments that they are to do a paper and prepare a presentation. I usually try to get students to present their work. This is a good practice for what they will do in the business world. Most of the time, they will be required to prepare an analysis and present it. If you don't have the class time or inclination to have the students present, then you can of course cut out the aspect of them putting together a presentation.

If you want to point students toward highly ranked journals in AI, here's a list of the top journals as reported by *various citation counts sources* (this list changes year to year):

o   Communications of the ACM

o   Artificial Intelligence

o   Cognitive Science

o   IEEE Transactions on Pattern Analysis and Machine Intelligence

o   Foundations and Trends in Machine Learning

o   Journal of Memory and Language

o   Cognitive Psychology

o   Neural Networks

o   IEEE Transactions on Neural Networks and Learning Systems

o   IEEE Intelligent Systems

o   Knowledge-based Systems

GUIDE TO USING THE CHAPTERS

For each of the chapters, I provide next some various ways to use the chapter material. You can assign the tasks as individual homework assignments, or the tasks can be used with team projects for the class. You can easily layout a series of assignments, such as indicating that the students are to do item "a" below for say Chapter 1, then "b" for the next chapter of the book, and so on.

a) What is the main point of the chapter and describe in your own words the significance of the topic,

b) Identify at least two aspects in the chapter that you agree with, and support your concurrence by providing at least one other outside researched item as support; make sure to explain your basis for disagreeing with the aspects,

c) Identify at least two aspects in the chapter that you disagree with, and support your disagreement by providing at least one other outside researched item as support; make sure to explain your basis for disagreeing with the aspects,

d) Find an aspect that was not covered in the chapter, doing so by conducting outside research, and then explain how that aspect ties into the chapter and what significance it brings to the topic,

e) Interview a specialist in industry about the topic of the chapter, collect from them their thoughts and opinions, and readdress the chapter by citing your source and how they compared and contrasted to the material,

f) Interview a relevant academic professor or researcher in a college or university about the topic of the chapter, collect from them their thoughts and opinions, and readdress the chapter by citing your source and how they compared and contrasted to the material,

g) Try to update a chapter by finding out the latest on the topic, and ascertain whether the issue or topic has now been solved or whether it is still being addressed, explain what you come up with.

The above are all ways in which you can get the students of your class involved in considering the material of a given chapter. You could mix things up by having one of those above assignments per each week, covering the chapters over the course of the semester or quarter.

As a reminder, here are the chapters of the book and you can select whichever chapters you find most valued for your particular class:

Chapter Title

Companion Book By This Author

Advances in AI and Autonomous Vehicles: Cybernetic Self-Driving Cars

Practical Advances in Artificial Intelligence (AI) and Machine Learning

by

Dr. Lance B. Eliot, MBA, PhD

This title is available via Amazon and other book sellers

Companion Book By This Author

Self-Driving Cars:
"The Mother of All AI Projects"

by Dr. Lance B. Eliot, MBA, PhD

This title is available via Amazon and other book sellers

Companion Book By This Author

Innovation and Thought Leadership on Self-Driving Driverless Cars

by Dr. Lance B. Eliot, MBA, PhD

This title is available via Amazon and other book sellers

This title is available via Amazon and other book sellers

Companion Book By This Author

Introduction to Driverless Self-Driving Cars

by Dr. Lance B. Eliot, MBA, PhD

Chapter Title

This title is available via Amazon and other book sellers

Companion Book By This Author
Autonomous Vehicle Driverless Self-Driving Cars and Artificial Intelligence
by Dr. Lance B. Eliot, MBA, PhD

This title is available via Amazon and other book sellers

Companion Book By This Author

Transformative Artificial Intelligence Driverless Self-Driving Cars

by Dr. Lance B. Eliot, MBA, PhD

This title is available via Amazon and other book sellers

<u>Companion Book By This Author</u>

***Disruptive Artificial Intelligence
and Driverless Self-Driving Cars***

by Dr. Lance B. Eliot, MBA, PhD

<u>Chapter Title</u>

This title is available via Amazon and other book sellers

Companion Book By This Author

State-of-the-Art
AI Driverless Self-Driving Cars

by Dr. Lance B. Eliot, MBA, PhD

Chapter Title

This title is available via Amazon and other book sellers

Companion Book By This Author

Top Trends in AI Self-Driving Cars

by Dr. Lance B. Eliot, MBA, PhD

This title is available via Amazon and other book sellers

<u>Companion Book By This Author</u>

AI Innovations
and Self-Driving Cars

by Dr. Lance B. Eliot, MBA, PhD

<u>Chapter Title</u>

This title is available via Amazon and other book sellers

ABOUT THE AUTHOR

Dr. Lance B. Eliot, MBA, PhD is the CEO of Techbruim, Inc. and Executive Director of the Cybernetic Self-Driving Car Institute, and has over twenty years of industry experience including serving as a corporate officer in a billion dollar firm and was a partner in a major executive services firm. He is also a serial entrepreneur having founded, ran, and sold several high-tech related businesses. He previously hosted the popular radio show *Technotrends* that was also available on American Airlines flights via their in-flight audio program. Author or co-author of a dozen books and over 400 articles, he has made appearances on CNN, and has been a frequent speaker at industry conferences.

A former professor at the University of Southern California (USC), he founded and led an innovative research lab on Artificial Intelligence in Business. Known as the "AI Insider" his writings on AI advances and trends has been widely read and cited. He also previously served on the faculty of the University of California Los Angeles (UCLA), and was a visiting professor at other major universities. He was elected to the International Board of the Society for Information Management (SIM), a prestigious association of over 3,000 high-tech executives worldwide.

He has performed extensive community service, including serving as Senior Science Adviser to the Vice Chair of the Congressional Committee on Science & Technology. He has served on the Board of the OC Science & Engineering Fair (OCSEF), where he is also has been a Grand Sweepstakes judge, and likewise served as a judge for the Intel International SEF (ISEF). He served as the Vice Chair of the Association for Computing Machinery (ACM) Chapter, a prestigious association of computer scientists. Dr. Eliot has been a shark tank judge for the USC Mark Stevens Center for Innovation on start-up pitch competitions, and served as a mentor for several incubators and accelerators in Silicon Valley and Silicon Beach. He served on several Boards and Committees at USC, including having served on the Marshall Alumni Association (MAA) Board in Southern California.

Dr. Eliot holds a PhD from USC, MBA, and Bachelor's in Computer Science, and earned the CDP, CCP, CSP, CDE, and CISA certifications. Born and raised in Southern California, and having traveled and lived internationally, he enjoys scuba diving, surfing, and sailing.

ADDENDUM

Crucial Advances for AI Driverless Cars

Practical Advances in Artificial Intelligence (AI) and Machine Learning

By

Dr. Lance B. Eliot, MBA, PhD

———

For supplemental materials of this book, visit:

www.ai-selfdriving-cars.guru

For special orders of this book, contact:

LBE Press Publishing

Email: LBE.Press.Publishing@gmail.com

www.ingramcontent.com/pod-product-compliance
Lightning Source LLC
Chambersburg PA
CBHW051232050326
40689CB00007B/900